"Norman Beim ranks with the best in America today."

-- WHBI RADIO

ON A DARKLING PLAIN:
"...a comedy-drama in the best sense, with both comic and dramatic sides complementing and enriching each other...a must see."

-- THE DAILY OKLAHOMAN

"The characters are richly drawn and the plot is cleverly woven."

-- LEAH POSLUNS THEATRE, TORONTO

"...a tense, realistic drama with rounded characters...a meaningful story in poignant detail."

-- THE SCRIPT REVIEW

SHAKESPEARE REVISITED:
"Intelligent, right-to-the-jugular..."

-- BUFFALO ART VOICE

DREAMS:
"Lunt and Fontanne would have loved it...a lovely, poignant play."

-- DON LEVY, LODI ARTS COMMISSION

INSIDE:
"...very successfully presented at the Provincetown Playhouse...an unusual comedy which had the audience in an uproar."

-- THE VILLAGER, NEW YORK CITY

THE DESERTER:
"The Deserter by Norman Beim and the Great Nebula in Orion by Lanford Wilson are theatrical gems, each cracking with its own electricity...(The Deserter) a powerful moving piece of art...heart-wrenching portrayal of the soldier is sensitive but not maudlin...the audience is enveloped in the tense emotional drama."

-- THE TARGUM, RUTGERS UNIVERSITY

SIX AWARD WINNING PLAYS

Norman Beim

NEWCONCEPT
press, inc.
Emerson New Jersey

Samuel French, Inc.
45 West 25th Street
New York, New York 10010

Library of Congress Cataloging-in-Publication Data

Beim, Norman.
Six award winning plays / Norman Beim.
p. cm.
Contents: On a darkling plain -- Shakespeare revisited -- Dreams -- Inside -- Jewel thieves! -- The deserter.
ISBN 0-931231-06-X (alk. paper)
I. Title. II. Title: Six award winning plays.
PS3552.E4224A13 1995
812'.54--dc20 94-40724
CIP

Special thanks to LARRY ERLBAUM, ART LIZZA, FRANK BARA, DAVID LAWLOR, ARTHUR TOBIAS, VINCE BUMB, and last, but not least, MARTY BEIM.

Printed in the United States of America

10 9 8 7 6 5 4 3 2

Contents

For Gloria Slatin
who generously loaned me her pen knife.

Preface

I was in combat, as part of the ammunition squad in the field artillery, when I received word that my one-act, INSIDE, had won second prize in a nation-wide competition sponsored by the New England Theatre Conference. (I think that was the name of the organization. It was a long time ago.) There was a check enclosed . . . for twenty five dollars. My first serious effort as a writer had been recognized, not only recognized but honored. Perhaps there was a God, after all, and maybe I would come out of this hellish war alive. Perhaps I was really destined for greatness.

INSIDE was written at Camp Pickett, Virginia. I was facing war at the time and the imminent possibility of death. I thought back on my childhood, which was not that far back, and I recalled the happy times, especially those enchanted hours I spent in the local library. Our branch library was a charming lawn-fronted, ivy-covered, two story building. Upstairs was the children's department and downstairs the adult department. I relived my visits to that magical sanctuary, which usually took place on a Saturday morning. In my imagination I roamed the book-shelves in the person of seven different people . . . schizophrenia taken to the extreme.

A formal plot was unthinkable. Crass, crude, commercial! My first and, perhaps, my only effort must be a poetic work. Not necessarily verse. Essences . . . that was what I was after . . . and the truth, as

I saw it. Dialogue, per se, was frivolous. That was what you heard on the radio, and in the movies. I was going to go inside the hearts and minds of my characters and verbalize their most private thoughts.

The writing took place in the camp library, in the evening, after basic training. What a gargantuan effort! Juggling three, four, five, six, seven different personalities. After three laborious hours of concentrated effort I was lucky if I produced half a page and I was exhausted. An absolutely wrenching experience!

When it was finished I was completely drained . . . with very mixed feelings. It was a clumsy piece. It was an inspired work. It was pedestrian, not nearly close enough to my inspiration. But it was the best I could do and I sent it off to the competition.

Jasper Deeter at Hedgerow Theatre outside of Philadelphia, where I was studying acting after the war, expressed enthusiasm for INSIDE and threatened several times to include it in the repertory, but never did. The play finally had its premiere at the legendary Provincetown Playhouse in Greenwich Village in New York City, where I had come to find my fortune as an actor. It was produced by The Journeyman, a theatre group composed of journalists, and directed imaginatively by a young actor named Michael Simone. The production received an excellent review and was followed by a student production at Columbia University and a couple of local productions, one of which I directed.

My war experiences at an early age brought me down to earth with a thud. Riding through a devastated Germany, bodies lying along the road. (Were they Germans or Americans?) Rolling into the snow-covered Hurtgen Forest during the Battle of The Bulge and receiving word that the first man to be killed in our unit was the kindest and gentlest of souls. Trying to dig a fox-hole in the frozen earth. Urinating in our helmets because it was too cold to get up. Wandering lost in the dark in the early hours of the morning, having lost contact with my squad on the way to Belgium to pick up ammunition. Listening to the shells flying overhead. Maybe being a successful novelist with a penthouse on Park Avenue, and a beautiful woman who looked like the movie-star, Hedy LaMarr, at my side, was not to be.

The cruelty of life shook me up a bit, so that when I read William Bradford Huie's book about Private Eddie Slovik, the only American soldier executed for desertion during World War II, I felt it spoke to me personally. I had qualms about bearing arms and killing my fellow man. "Thou shalt not kill," the Bible said. How ironic that morality can be twisted to suit the times. I was deeply moved by Eddie Slovik's story.

By this time I was reduced to writing ordinary, pedestrian dialogue . . . anything to get out the passionate thoughts and feelings bottled up inside of me. The plan for the play was a simple one. Too simple, I feared. But it came from the heart and to hell with dramatic structure which I'd been studying so intensely. Eddie Slovik, The Soldier, is brought to a deserted chateau in France by a guard, given his last rites by a priest and led off to his execution. Without my being aware of it the play contained the most essential dramatic element of all, conflict. Conflict between Eddie and the guard, conflict between Eddie and the priest . . . and I tried to be fair to all.

I was then part of an Off-Off-Broadway theatre called The Troupe, located on West 39th Street in New York City. The Troupe was established in a collapsed three story building, which was practically single handedly restored to use by an anomaly named Andy Milligan. His was a thorny, irascible nature and he succeeded in alienating many, but somehow I managed to gain his favor and we got along well, for the most part. I grew very fond of Andy, admired his guts and found his misogyny rather amusing.

Andy could do anything . . . build houses, write screen plays and then produce, direct and edit them. (His horror films had a cult following both here in the States and in Europe.) Andy designed costumes (he once had his own dress shop). He was an actor, a carpenter, an electrician, a playwright . . . you name it. He was also a veteran of Cafe Cino, a legendary Greenwich Village theatre where anyone was free to get up and do his or her own thing. Cafe Cino produced such artists as the playwright Lanford Wilson and the director Marshall Mason.

The top floor of The Troupe was Andy's living quarters, his and his cat, Trouper. The first floor was a large black box. Chairs were placed wherever desired. The second floor was a tiny proscenium theatre seating forty or so. The building was freezing in the winter and roasting in the summer, and the equipment, to put it mildly, was crude. The spaces were available free of charge to anyone with a project. Most of the time there were four productions going on at once. The box office take, what there was of it, went to the maintenance of the building. Utility bills were always long overdue and there was always the threat of the electricity being turned off, or the public phone in the hallway being removed. Andy was always desperately seeking to sell more shares in the building to the limited number of share-holders, nineteen I believe, in order to pay expenses. I bought a half share . . . as a charitable contribution. It was really more than I could afford. Andy eventually sold the building and moved to California to continue to produce his horror films. Ironically the shares paid off at an unbelievable rate. If only I could have afforded to buy more.

THE DESERTER, Eddie Slovik's story, was written out of the agony of my war experiences. The running time was half an hour, and I directed a production of it at The Troupe, in the tiny theatre on the second floor, in the dead of winter, as part of a bill of one-acts of mine. We played twelve performances, as an Equity showcase. Once there were exactly two people in the audience. However a radio critic attended one performance and gave the evening a rave review.

The role of Eddie Slovik, The Soldier, was played by a talented actor named Jim Stubbs who, to my admiration and envy, could shed real tears. I hesitated to ask him to pick up the pace when I saw such concrete evidence of his deep emotion.

I entered THE DESERTER in a competition sponsored by the Double Image Theatre and Samuel French, publishers. It won the competition and was published by Samuel French in an acting edition. The finals of the competition was attended by Marshall Mason, who by that time had founded Circle Rep. Marshall subsequently produced THE DESERTER at Circle Rep with John Bard Manulis, now a film producer, as director. THE DESERTER continues to be produced around the country.

An acquaintance of mine invited me to a performance of a comedy whose leading characters were supposedly based on Alfred Lunt and Lynn Fontanne. The Lunts, as they were commonly known, were great stars of the American Theatre and, along with Noel Coward and Gertrude Lawrence, were among my idols. I found the comedy superficial, with no feeling at all for what I thought the Lunts were like. At that time my parents were past middle age and my father, in particular, was ailing. I wondered what it must be like to leave forever a partner with whom one had shared most of one's life. Death, of course, is something we all ponder.

I had read much about the Lunts and proceeded to write a play whose lives closely resembled theirs. The two characters, however, were placed in a fictional situation. They were coming out of retirement when one of them is suddenly faced with the threat of the final curtain. Some of the play was lots of fun to write; some of it was painful. DREAMS was my personal valentine to the theatre and I doubted if it would appeal to many.

The positive response was a pleasant surprise. I got a phone call from a producer in Florida I'd submitted the play to, telling me how much he liked my play. A Broadway producer offered the script to several first rank stars. I, myself, submitted the play to some stars, most of whom responded warmly . . . but no commitment. One star even graciously consented to sit around her apartment and read the script aloud for me. I suggested we ask her husband, an actor of some reknown, to read opposite her. She then offered to hold readings for producers and backers, but her husband had read so badly I found myself in a quandry. Should I go ahead and take a chance on the husband improving? He was an experienced actor. But suppose he didn't? It was, for all intents and purposes, a two character play. Could I suggest we replace him? Would she be offended? If we used their apartment, he would be present and that, certainly, would be embarrassing. It was a situation I just couldn't cope with so I let the opportunity slip by.

DREAMS won a play competition sponsored by the No Empty Space Theatre on Staten Island, which presented me with a nice little check. I was recently flown to Lansing, Michigan by the Boarshead Theatre for a staged reading of the play.

Social injustice has alternately pained me and made me fighting mad. I lived through the McCarthy era and the black-listing, but since I was not a Communist, nor had I made the mistake of being at the wrong place at the wrong time and, luckily, my name was not confused with someone on the wrong list, I was never personally affected by the witch hunt. However I had fumed and agonized about the people whose lives had been ruined during those years.

I wrote a play called THE PRIVATE AGONY OF LEONARD COHN, but wasn't very happy with it and put it aside. Years later I took it out of the drawer and rewrote it from a more philosophical view. It still dealt with the bitterness of those years but now I focused on the healing of old wounds. What did revenge accomplish? Was there really such a thing as vengeance?

Playwrights Preview Productions, a New York City group, scheduled a reading of the play, now called ON A DARKLING PLAIN. The title was taken from a line in Matthew Arnold's lovely poem, DOVER BEACH. I directed the reading and cast a talented veteran, Martin Rudy, in the role of the black-listed actor. After looking over the script, Marty suggested that the antagonist, who never appeared in the play, should have at least a scene or two. Two powerful scenes in the play came about as a result of his suggestion.

I was also flown to Toronto for a staged reading of the play by the Leah Posluns Theatre and it also received a staged reading at the

Jewish Ensemble Theatre outside of Detroit. ON A DARKLING PLAIN was produced simultaneously by The Street Players Theatre in Norman, Oklahoma, where it received excellent reviews, and Theatre Americana in Altadena, California where it won the David James Ellis Memorial Award as best play of the season, and its leading actor was singled out for giving the best performance of the season.

The comedy-mystery films of the nineteen thirties and forties have always intrigued me. The sophisticated shenanigans of William Powell and Kay Francis. Marlene Dietrich stealing pearls. JEWEL THIEVES! was written just for the fun of it, an airy piece of fluff. It won a new play competition conducted by the Ferndale Repertory Theatre and I flew up to Ferndale, in northern California, for its premiere. Ferndale is a charming town . . . more like a village . . . similar to Provincetown on Cape Cod. It has many Victorian houses and the theatre put me up in a quaint, turn of the century hotel.

Comedy, on the surface, seems so simple . . . simple to write and simple to perform, and yet it happens to be most difficult. And there are so few American actors with a sense of high style, which actually demands more intensity, not less . . . and, God help me, diction.

Many people in the American theatre feel America has a right to its own parochial approach to Shakespeare and, of late, it's become the vogue to cast ethnic actors in all sorts of roles, whether they're suited to them or not. History and logic are thrown aside in an attempt to atone for social injustice. This system of color-blind casting provoked me to write SHAKESPEARE REVISITED, in which Shakespeare comes down to earth and views a production of RICHARD III which contains some odd bits of casting. SHAKESPEARE REVISITED won the one-act division of the Maxim Mazumdar new play competition sponsored by the Alleyway Theatre in Buffalo, New York where it had its premiere. The following year I enjoyed playing the role of Shakespeare in a local New York production.

Norman Beim

ON A DARKLING PLAIN

A Comedy-Drama in Two Acts

Ah, love, let us be true
To one another! for the world, which seems
To lie before us like a land of dreams,
So various, so beautiful, so new,
Hath really neither joy, nor love, nor light,
Nor certitude, nor peace, nor help for pain;
And we are here as on a darkling plain
Swept with confused alarms of struggle
and flight,
Where ignorant armies clash by night.

Matthew Arnold
DOVER BEACH

CAST OF CHARACTERS

Miriam Leonard
Jerry Miller
Guy Leonard
George Makapoulos

SCENE

The upper West Side apartment
of the Leonard family in New York City.

TIME

Act One:
Scene One. Friday Noon, January, 1964.
Scene Two. That evening.

Act Two:
Scene One. The action is continuous.
Scene Two. The following Sunday afternoon.

ACT I

Scene 1

(The adjoining breakfast room and living room of the Leonard apartment in New York City. Though the apartment is spacious and well furnished the furniture has obviously seen better days. MIRIAM LEONARD, a pleasant looking woman pushing fifty, enters the breakfast room from the kitchen with a glass of orange juice, which she places on the table and goes back into the kitchen. GUY LEONARD, a well built, impressive looking man about fifty, enters from the bedroom, crosses through the living room and sits down at the table. HE's wearing pajamas and a robe and looks like he just got out of bed. HE proceeds to drink his orange juice. MIRIAM re-enters from the kitchen with a bowl of oatmeal which SHE places on the table in front of GUY. GUY pours some milk on the oatmeal, adds sugar and eats his oatmeal as MIRIAM returns to the kitchen and re-enters with a pot of coffee. SHE pours two cups, one for GUY and one for herself, returns the pot to the kitchen, re-enters and sits opposite GUY.)

GUY: Guess who I had in my cab last night.

MIRIAM: Mahatma Ghandi.

GUY: Close. Ernie Buttram. You remember Ernie. He was the one that produced "Blue Sunday," and that little western that I did. What was the name of it?

MIRIAM: You're asking me?

GUY: "The Vanishing Horseman." That was it. "The Vanishing Horseman." God, I had a lot of fun on that one. I had to learn to ride. Remember?

MIRIAM: What did Ernie have to say?

GUY: "Keep the change." I picked him up in the Village. When he got into the cab he didn't realize who I was, until, of course, he saw my picture on the license. You should have seen his face. I was watching him in my mirror. He turned all colors, sank back into the seat and buried himself behind a magazine. When we got to the Plaza he jumped out so fast I thought for sure he was gonna fall on his face. He shoves a five dollar bill at me, mumbles "Keep the change," and he was gone. The change came to exactly one fat dime.

MIRIAM: Isn't he the one we almost ran into on Fifth Avenue? He crossed the street to avoid running into us.

GUY: That was Dick Wendell. He was the one that directed "Blue Sunday."

MIRIAM: Yes, of course, Richard Wendell. Didn't you get him that job?

GUY: I recommended him, when the first director got sick.

MIRIAM: I used to feed him twice a week and you gave him two of your suits.

GUY: And some money, which he never repaid. However, I will say this for Dick. He has been using some blacklisted writers.

MIRIAM: Because he can get them cheap.

GUY: Quite possibly.

MIRIAM: And he's never called you even once.

GUY: Yes, well, I guess I'd have to change my face as well as my name.

MIRIAM: (*After a moment.*) Kenny's been accepted by Harvard.

GUY: That's wonderful.

MIRIAM: It came in the morning mail. He may not go, he said.

GUY: What do you mean, he may not go?

MIRIAM: He's worried about the money. Do you know what a year at Harvard costs?

GUY: That's my affair.

MIRIAM: Where are you gonna get that kind of money? We've borrowed from the family. Both yours and mine. We've taken a loan on this apartment. Okay, okay. That's your affair. (*Feeling her way.*) George called last night.

GUY: George?

MIRIAM: Yes, George.

GUY: You mean George Makapoulos?

MIRIAM: No, George Washington.

GUY: (*Contempt and curiosity.*) What did George have to say?

MIRIAM: He wants you for the play. He said that if you sign for the play you'll be guaranteed the film as well.

GUY: Are you quite sure of that?

MIRIAM: That's what he said.

GUY: I thought the play was cast.

MIRIAM: Apparently not.

GUY: They go into rehearsal next week.

MIRIAM: He left a number for you to call.

GUY: Did you talk to him?

MIRIAM: I took the message.

GUY: He called me personally?

MIRIAM: That's what I said.

GUY: Does he really think that I could ever possibly work with him again?

MIRIAM: Apparently.

GUY: Amazing. Absolutely amazing. What else did he have to say?

MIRIAM: He asked how you were. He asked about the kids and I asked about Jenny. She was operated on, you know.

GUY: You had quite a little chat.

MIRIAM: Not really, no. I was civil to him.

GUY: You don't really think that I could—that I could even consider doing that play? Do you?

MIRIAM: Why not?

GUY: Why not? I suppose you approve of what Alfred did.

MIRIAM: I don't approve of the way he did it.

GUY: He sends me a copy of the script and then I pick up the New York Times and what do I read? "George Makapoulos to direct the new Alfred Matthews play." I still cannot believe it.

MIRIAM: He should have called you first.

GUY: He knew what I would say. You remember what he said? In this very room! He was sitting in that chair—where you're sitting now. "As far as I'm concerned," he said, "As far as I'm concerned George Makapoulos does not exist any longer."

MIRIAM: Maybe Alfred had no choice. I mean if George can guarantee the movie, there must be a movie tie-in somewhere, and maybe that's how they got together. I mean maybe the producer brought them both together.

GUY: There is always a choice. The question is does Alfred need a hit that badly.

MIRIAM: He's never had anything to match "The Day of Judgement."

GUY: So he thinks that if the three of us got together, lightning will strike again. (*HE grows reflective and smiles.*) Did I ever tell you how I first met George? It was in Myron's class. He was teaching then and I did a scene. I think it was a scene from "Waiting For Lefty." Anyway, after I sat down I noticed this strange young man with these dark piercing eyes. He kept staring at me. I thought he was going to bore a hole right through the back of my head. We take a break, and I go to the "john." This kid follows me in and stands right next to me, and I said to myself, "Oh, no! He's going to make a pass at me." And then he starts telling me what was wrong with my scene. I'm standing there taking a leak and this perfect stranger is trying to teach me how to act. Of course, everything he said was right on the button. And he wasn't a bad little actor. Except for the fact that he kept telling people what to do. I said to him one day, "For God sakes, George, why don't you teach acting?" He looked at me. "In a class?" he said. "You must be kidding!" Oh, yes indeed! George Makapoulos always knew where he was going. (*Bitterly.*) No matter what the price.

MIRIAM: In all fairness to George, he did come to us and tell us what he was going to do. And he promised to name only those that had been named already. And he even tried to persuade us to join him. I thought for sure he was going to have a nervous breakdown. How he ever got through all of that I shall never know.

GUY: Oh, he got through it all right, with a million dollar contract to help ease the pain.

MIRIAM: A three picture deal, as I recall.

GUY: Oh, I see. He did it for his art. Then that makes it all right. (*After a moment.*) God, how I loved that man! If he'd been a woman I would have married him. But what he did was shit.

MIRIAM: Yes. Well even shit dries up and blows away. I am not a fan of George Makapoulos. You know that. I have never been a fan of his.

GUY: You were jealous of him.

MIRIAM: Quite possibly. However, he did bring out the best in you—on the stage, that is.

GUY: And that's why you think I ought to do this play.

MIRIAM: Why do you think he's calling you? Out of the goodness of his heart? Because he loves you so much? He's calling you because he thinks that you're the best actor for the part. How many times have you worked with actors you despised? How many times have you worked with a director you had no respect for? Why do you shake your head?

GUY: Because I would have to shake his hand. And I'm afraid I couldn't do that.

MIRIAM: (*SHE smiles and speaks half to herself.*) "I'll never use that son of a bitch—unless I really need him."

GUY: What?

MIRIAM: Isn't that the old joke? "I'll never use that son of a bitch, unless I really need him." (*After a moment.*) You can close that bathroom door as much as you like, but I have heard you. I've heard you sobbing your heart out. Your career is slipping away from you, day by day, year by year and it's killing you.

GUY: I've held out this long. I can hold out a little bit longer.

MIRIAM: When Kenny leaves the house this Fall, the nest will be empty. Those kids are your security blanket. You'll have nothing to cling to anymore.

GUY: I'll have you.

MIRIAM: You're a talented man. You should be working. And you shouldn't have to settle for an occasional job somewhere in the wilds of Pennsylvania.

GUY: Franklin College is not the wilds of Pennsylvania.

MIRIAM: Alfred wrote that role for you.

GUY: That's not what he said. What he said was, "I had you in mind when I wrote that role." He's very cagey that way.

MIRIAM: Nevertheless they want you. Both the author and the director want you. It's a fine role in a fine play. In addition to that you'd get to play your role on the screen. What more could you ask for?

(GUY chuckles.)

MIRIAM: What's so funny?

GUY: You remember Myron Cohen, the nightclub comedian?

MIRIAM: What about him?

GUY: He used to tell this story about the Plotkin diamond. It was the most beautiful, the most valuable diamond in the world. The only trouble was the Plotkin diamond had a curse that came along with it.

MIRIAM: Mr. Plotkin. (*Urgently.*) You've got to let go. You've got to let go of the past. It's eating you up. And that box of letters. What are you saving them for? One of these days I'm going to take that box and burn it.

GUY: I thought you were gonna use those letters in that novel of yours. Incidentally, when are you gonna start on this mythical book of yours?

MIRIAM: Don't change the subject. You cannot afford to turn this down. I have George's number. He'll be home all week-end. Will you call him? Guy?

GUY: I'll think about it. (*HE rises.*)

MIRIAM: Where are you going?

GUY: I've gotta class to teach.

MIRIAM: You've got hours yet.

GUY: I've gotta shower, make myself pretty. That takes longer and longer. (*HE goes off toward the bedrooms.*)

(The doorbell rings. MIRIAM hesitates, then goes to the intercom and presses the buzzer.)

MIRIAM: Clarence? Clarence?

(The doorbell rings again. MIRIAM sighs, shakes her head and goes off through the living room to the foyer, Stage Left.)

MIRIAM: (*Offstage*). Come in, Jerry. Come in.

(A moment later JERRY MILLER, a nice looking man in his thirties, enters the living room, followed shortly by Miriam.)

MIRIAM: I wasn't expecting you this early.

JERRY: It's lunchtime, isn't it?

MIRIAM: We keep such crazy hours in this house.

JERRY: You look great!

MIRIAM: You sound so surprised.

JERRY: I'm sorry. I didn't mean it that way. I'm trying to remember when we saw each other last. It must have been at my parents' anniversary. You came with your little girl. And you have a son, as well.

MIRIAM: Kenny. He graduates high school in the Spring.

JERRY: I spent Thanksgiving with Carrie, you know.

MIRIAM: Yes. Yes, I know.

JERRY: She's turned out to be an excellent cook. I never knew that you wrote poetry. I came across your yearbook. According to Carrie you were going to be another Margaret Mitchell.

MIRIAM: Jane Austen, please.

JERRY: I don't suppose you've kept up with your writing.

MIRIAM: As a matter of fact, I did have one short story that was actually published. How about some lunch?

JERRY: I could use some coffee.

MIRIAM: Come with me.

JERRY: Where are we going?

MIRIAM: Into the breakfast room. Come. Sit down. Now, we have some meat loaf. Soup. I can make you some eggs.

JERRY: Just some coffee.

MIRIAM: How about a pecan roll?

JERRY: You twisted my arm.

MIRIAM: They're Guy's favorite.

(MIRIAM goes into the kitchen. JERRY is in the chair and looks about. As HE turns, the leg of the chair comes loose. HE rises and examines the chair as MIRIAM re-enters with a mug of coffee.)

JERRY: I'm breaking up your furniture.

MIRIAM: We need a new kitchen set. Just give it a smack. Or better yet, take another chair.

(SHE goes back into the kitchen. JERRY pushes the leg of the chair back into place and resumes his seat. HE puts milk and sugar into his coffee and takes a sip as MIRIAM re-enters with a pecan roll on a plate.)

JERRY: That looks great. Haven't had one in years.

MIRIAM: There's margarine, if you like. I understand that you're now a vice president.

JERRY: There are fifty vice presidents at Continental. How's your husband doing?

MIRIAM: Oh, he's just fine.

JERRY: I read in the paper just the other day about the Alfred Matthews play. Is he going to be in it?

MIRIAM: We're not quite sure.

JERRY: Mr. Makapoulos is directing it, isn't he?

MIRIAM: Yes. Yes, he is.

JERRY: Is Guy still driving a cab?

MIRIAM: That's the way we pay our bills. He also teaches a couple of acting classes.

JERRY: That's incredible. An actor of Guy Leonard's stature—driving a cab.

MIRIAM: Oh, he's done a couple shows. Last year he played King Lear at Franklin University.

JERRY: I was wondering—. Do you think he might be interested in doing a commercial for television? A number of stars are doing them now. Henry Fonda, for one. As a matter of fact, did you know that Eleanor Roosevelt did one? For Blue Bonnet margarine?

MIRIAM: No, I didn't know that.

JERRY: She gave the money to charity, of course. What do you think?

MIRIAM: I can't speak for Guy, but I know that he doesn't approve of stars doing commercials for television.

JERRY: They pay a lot of money, you know.

MIRIAM: Yes. Yes, I know.

JERRY: We're launching this new campaign. It's going to be a pretty big one. There's a lot of money involved. All that exposure. What do you think?

MIRIAM: I'm not his agent, Jerry. You'd have to speak to Guy about this.

JERRY: Is he in right now?

MIRIAM: (*Hesitantly.*) Yes. I'll let him know that you're here.

JERRY: Thank you.

(MIRIAM goes off toward the bedrooms. JERRY continues to eat his pecan roll and drinks his coffee. MIRIAM re-enters.)

MIRIAM: He'll be out shortly.

JERRY: Thank you.

MIRIAM: You know, of course, that Guy's been blacklisted. He hasn't worked in movies, on television or on radio for the past twelve years.

JERRY: I've spoken to several people at the agency about him. As a matter of fact it turned out that the president of Continental is a fan of his.

MIRIAM: I see. Why don't we go into the living room? I'm sorry. You haven't finished yet.

JERRY: That's quite all right. I've been snacking all morning.

(THEY adjourn to the living room.)

JERRY: I can't get used to all this space. How many rooms do you have?

MIRIAM: Seven, God help me.

JERRY: This place must cost a fortune.

MIRIAM: We bought it—a long time ago. Sit down, Jerry, please.

JERRY: Thank you. That's an excellent picture of Laurence Olivier. It's autographed, I see.

MIRIAM: He was here for dinner. He came to see Guy in "The Day of Judgement."

JERRY: I've never met him, you know. Guy, I mean.

MIRIAM: I thought you had.

JERRY: No, I never have. I almost went backstage when I saw "The Day of Judgement."

MIRIAM: Why didn't you?

JERRY: I don't know. I guess I felt it was kind of presumptuous of me. We're not even related.

MIRIAM: We're all related in one way or another, if you go back far enough.

(GUY enters in sports jacket, shirt and tie.)

MIRIAM: This is Jerry, Guy.

GUY: Yes, of course. You're Carrie's little brother.

JERRY: Well, not so little. How do you do, sir. It's a privilege to meet you, sir. (*HE shakes hands vigorously.*)

GUY: He's very polite.

MIRIAM: He's Jewish.

GUY: Sit down, Jerry.

JERRY: Thank you—.

MIRIAM: I've got some things to do. If you need anything just give a yell.

(MIRIAM goes to the breakfast room, stands concerned for a moment, sighs, then clears the table and takes the things into the kitchen.)

GUY: You're in advertising, I understand.

JERRY: Yes, I'm with Continental.

GUY: That's a big one.

JERRY: One of the biggest.

GUY: What, exactly, do you do?

JERRY: I write copy—for television commercials. As a matter of fact, that's one of the reasons I'm here. I'm working on a new campaign for Cotton Soft.

GUY: Toilet paper?

JERRY: It's not very glamorous, I know. But it is something everyone uses every day.

GUY: Hopefully.

JERRY: Yes, well—Cotton Soft has been around for years, and lately it hasn't been doing so well—so they're giving Continental a shot at it. As a matter of fact, it was my presentation that won them over. We've got this series of vignettes. Actually they're sort of miniature plays, and this one actor appears in all of them. In one, he's a laborer. In another he plays a druggist, a farmer, a lawyer. That sort of thing. What we need is an actor with enormous range. That's why I thought of you. You wouldn't have to hawk the product, or anything like that. All you'd have to do is to play these roles in these various little playlets.

GUY: What kind of playlets are they?

JERRY: Well, some of them are humorous. Some of them are sentimental. Human interest sort of things.

GUY: I see. How much does it pay?

JERRY: I—ah—really couldn't say.

GUY: A hundred? A thousand? A million?

JERRY: Well, it's certainly well over a thousand. I guess it would all depend on how much your agent negotiates.

GUY: I don't have an agent at the moment.

JERRY: As I understand it there's a session fee and this session fee is sort of an advance on your residuals. Your residuals, of course, would depend on how long and how frequently the spot is played.

GUY: A ball park figure.

JERRY: Well right now we've got two spots scheduled to shoot, I'd say maybe forty thousand. That would be an advance, you understand.

GUY: Is that for the two of them?

JERRY: Quite possibly. I really don't get involved in that end of it.

GUY: Have you some copy with you?

JERRY: Yes! Yes, I have! (*HE goes to the foyer and returns with his attache case.*) These are the two spots we'll be shooting first. That's the druggist. And that's the cab driver.

GUY: (*HE smiles.*) The cab driver?

JERRY: Yes. And these are the story boards. That's the commercials laid out in picture form. They give you an idea of the various shots.

GUY: I see. I like this one.

JERRY: That's the druggist.

GUY: I like that twist at the end. The girl's his daughter, I gather.

JERRY: Right.

GUY: Very clever.

JERRY: Thank you. Why don't I give you my card. (*Gives him his card.*) We're between fifty-fifth and fifty-sixth streets.

GUY: (*Reads the card.*) Vice president.

JERRY: It's no big deal, we're seeing people this afternoon starting at three. We'll be there till five-thirty—six o'clock.

GUY: I teach a class this afternoon.

JERRY: What time is your class?

GUY: Well, we start at two and we usually go till five—five-thirty.

JERRY: We'll be there till six.

GUY: And I'm all the way down in the Village.

JERRY: If you should decide to come and you think you're going to be late give us a ring.

GUY: Let me think about it, Jerry.

JERRY: (*Pressing the matter.*) Well, actually we're pretty much winding things up this afternoon. The fact of the matter is we've been casting this spot for quite some time now. As a matter of fact we'd pretty much decided on this one actor.

GUY: Oh? And who might that be?

JERRY: Jason Potts. Do you know him?

GUY: New England.

JERRY: Exactly. The fact of the matter is I gave your name to the casting department a couple of weeks ago. They've been trying to locate you through the various agents. They even called the Coast. And then this morning when I didn't see your name on the list I thought I'd better get in touch with you.

GUY: Did you write these spots?

JERRY: The idea is mine. And well, yes, for all intents and purposes.

GUY: How about a drink?

JERRY: Well, I—.

GUY: Please, won't you join me?

JERRY: Well, I guess it's just about martini time.

GUY: Is Scotch all right?

JERRY: Scotch is fine. Thank you. To better days. (*HE looks embarrassed.*)

GUY: (*Smiles.*) To better days.

(THEY drink.)

JERRY: Have you ever done a commercial, Guy?

GUY: On radio, a number of years ago—when I was first starting out.

JERRY: But never on TV.

GUY: No. No, never.

JERRY: A number of stars are doing them now.

GUY: Tell me something, Jerry.

JERRY: Yes, sir?

GUY: Have you been authorized to contact me?

JERRY: Well, I—

GUY: You're aware, of course, that I've been blacklisted. I haven't been able to work on television, radio or in the movies for the past twelve years.

JERRY: This is nineteen sixty-four.

GUY: In twenty years from now it will be nineteen eighty-four.

JERRY: I assure you, Guy—.

GUY: Don't. I was a Communist, you know. A card carrying Red.

JERRY: I knew that you took the "Fifth."

GUY: I took the "Fifth" at the advice of my attorney. I was told that if I didn't take the "Fifth" and admitted that I'd been a Communist I would have had to name names. And I just couldn't do that.

JERRY: What would have happened if you refused? To name names, I mean.

GUY: Fine and imprisonment.

JERRY: I see. Are you still—?

GUY: A member of the party? I don't know if the Communist party exists any longer, as a party, that is. I joined the party in the early thirties. That was the thing to do just then—for those that really cared about what was happening in the world. I attended five—six meetings. Maybe it was seven, I don't remember exactly, and then I quit.

JERRY: Why was that?

GUY: I found that I didn't have the time nor the energy to be both an actor and a politician. Then just a few years later Communism became a dirty word. Lillian Hellman put it beautifully. "I will not cut my conscience," she said, "to fit this year's fashions."

JERRY: Do you still believe in Communism?

GUY: Isn't Social Security a form of Communism? Isn't Medicare? And I think that most of us believe in some sort of national health. The only place I think you'll find Communism today, in its purest form, that is, is in a kibbutz in Israel. If you're asking me do I believe in the violent overthrow of the government, no, son, I am not a man of violence. Though it does appear that this country seems to thrive on it.

JERRY: Then you're a Socialist like Bernard Shaw.

(GUY does not respond. JERRY rises.)

JERRY: I'd better be getting back to the office. I do hope to see you this afternoon. You see we've got to make our decision by this weekend. The studio's booked for Tuesday.

GUY: That doesn't give you very much time.

JERRY: We have first refusal on Jason Potts.

GUY: I see.

JERRY: I've gotta get going. (*HE goes to the breakfast room doorway.*) Mimi?

(MIRIAM enters from the kitchen through the breakfast room.)

MIRIAM: You're leaving?

JERRY: I'm on my lunch hour. Hours. (*HE kisses her on the cheek.*)

MIRIAM: It's good to see you, Jerry, after all these years. You must have dinner with us some Sunday?

JERRY: Sounds good to me. It's been a pleasure meeting you, Guy. I do hope you can make it. (*HE shakes hands with GUY and follows MIRIAM.*) I guess you keep in touch with Carrie.

MIRIAM: I spoke to her this morning.

JERRY: Yes, I know. She may be coming into town next week.

(MIRIAM and JERRY go off to the foyer. GUY sits studying the copy, then sets them down and sips his drink. MIRIAM re-enters.)

MIRIAM: You're drinking kind of early, aren't you?

GUY: What's that? I was just being hospitable. I'm not gonna finish the bottle.

MIRIAM: In that case—. (*SHE puts the bottle away.*) What did Jerry have to say?

GUY: He's interested in me for a commercial.

MIRIAM: And what did you tell him?

GUY: I told him that I'd think about it.

MIRIAM: I thought you had no respect for actors who did commercials.

GUY: I never said that.

MIRIAM: I beg your pardon—stars. And what, pray tell, are you?

GUY: I drive a cab.

MIRIAM: On Broadway you're a star.

GUY: Actually it's a series of commercials. They're looking for someone to play these various roles—sort of an Everyman.

MIRIAM: Is this the copy? (*SHE picks up one of the sheets and glances through it.*)

GUY: They're quite well written. Don't you think?

MIRIAM: Do you know what the product is?

GUY: I've just been asked to audition.

MIRIAM: For toilet paper? You're not going to audition for this, are you?

GUY: I haven't decided yet. Look, my dear, even if I do decide to audition that doesn't mean they're going to offer it to me. And even if they offer it to me that doesn't mean that I have to accept it.

MIRIAM: Isn't that the idea of an audition? To get the job?

GUY: Not necessarily. They usually put these things on tape. It would give me a chance to get in front of a camera again.

MIRIAM: And what would that accomplish?

GUY: It would give me a chance to exercise certain muscles, which, for all I know, may have atrophied by now.

MIRIAM: When are they holding these auditions?

GUY: This afternoon.

MIRIAM: You're teaching a class this afternoon.

GUY: They'll be there till six.

MIRIAM: I see.

GUY: Jerry gave my name to the casting department. And he did take the trouble to come here personally. I think that the least I can do is to show up. Don't you?

MIRIAM: No. Not unless you intend to take the job. As a matter of fact, I think it would be dishonest—to lead people on like that. I really think you've gone out of your mind.

GUY: Look, Sweetie, I have absolutely no desire to do a commercial, much less a commercial for toilet paper.

MIRIAM: Suppose they offer it to you?

GUY: Let's take it one step at a time.

MIRIAM: If Jerry went to all this trouble, he must think that you're right for this—thing. So it stands to reason that if you do decide to audition there's an excellent chance that they will offer it to you. And if they offer it to you—you will end up accepting it.

GUY: I've just told you—.

MIRIAM: I know what you just told me—and I know you.

GUY: Now what is that supposed to mean?

MIRIAM: You are weak.

GUY: Would you repeat that please?

MIRIAM: You heard me.

GUY: I am weak. For ten long years I've been working my ass off. Driving that fucking cab for sixteen hours a day. Single-handedly I have succeeded in raising two beautiful children. Against insurmountable odds. For almost twenty-five years I have serviced—and satisfactorily, I trust—.

MIRIAM: Mmmmm—. (*SHE shrugs, holding her hand out and wiggling it from side to side.*)

GUY: One sex-starved Jewess and you've got the gall to tell me that I am weak?

MIRIAM: Let's put it this way. You are easily seduced.

GUY: You mean sexually.

MIRIAM: Sexually—.

GUY: All right, so I slipped a couple of times.

MIRIAM: A couple of times?! I'm just lucky that you never brought anything home.

GUY: If I'm so weak—I still can't believe that you said it—if I'm such a monster why did you take me back?

MIRIAM: You want to know why?

GUY: You couldn't bear to live without me.

MIRIAM: I came to the realization that you were really not responsible. That you are merely a product of your environment.

GUY: Here we go again.

MIRIAM: The product of a chauvinistic society where it's perfectly all right for a man to go out and "tear off a piece"—.

GUY: Such language from a nice Jewish girl!

MIRIAM: Am I right or am I wrong?

GUY: I never said that. Never! However—.

MIRIAM: Aha!

GUY: If there is such a thing as a double standard there happens to be a very good reason for it.

MIRIAM and GUY: A man cannot get pregnant.

MIRIAM: Does that mean that a man is not responsible? Does that mean that a man has no duty to Society? And besides in this day and age that argument does not hold water anymore.

GUY: I've gotta go.

MIRIAM: Who's stopping you?

(GUY goes off toward the bedrooms. MIRIAM sighs and studies the copy. GUY re-enters with his overcoat.)

GUY: You really are a snob. This is America you know! The land of free enterprise.

MIRIAM: Just the other day—what was it you said? Ah, yes. "Life is too short," you said. "From now on I'm going to do only the things that I really want to do."

GUY: Like drive a cab?

MIRIAM: I don't know where you're rushing to. You've got another hour yet.

GUY: I'm gonna take a bus. Come, give Daddy a kiss.

(SHE gives him a cursory peck.)

GUY: You call that a kiss?

MIRIAM: It's better than a kick in the ass.

(HE starts off.)

MIRIAM: What about dinner? Guy?

GUY: I'll give you a ring.

MIRIAM: When?

GUY: Whenever we take a break.

MIRIAM: What time is that?

GUY: Three-thirty—four. (*HE starts off again and comes back to her.*)

MIRIAM: What now?

GUY: It just occurred to me—.

MIRIAM: What?

GUY: We've got the house all to ourselves. All week-end long.

MIRIAM: (*Sarcastically.*) Hot diggety.

(HE sighs and strides off toward the foyer. MIRIAM hesitates, then calls out.)

MIRIAM: Guy? Guy??

(A door slam is heard.)

MIRIAM: Shit!

(SHE sighs and starts for the breakfast room.)

END OF ACT I, Scene 1

ACT I

Scene 2

(That evening. GUY is seated at the table in the breakfast room, glancing over a letter taken from a box in front of him. HE tosses the letter back into the box, goes to the phone and dials.)

GUY: Hello? Hello, Marge, it's Guy. I was just wondering—. Have you seen Mimi, by any chance? No, no Everything's fine. I just came home a little while ago and she isn't in. She probably went out to do some last minute shopping. Right. Right, thank you. (*HE hangs up, sighs, resumes his seat and picks up another letter from the box, then looks up.*) Mimi? Mimi??

(MIRIAM enters from the foyer.)

MIRIAM: No. It's Audrey Hepburn. Where are you?

GUY: I'm in the breakfast room. Where have you been?

MIRIAM: Out. (*SHE puts the cover back on the box, tosses the box into a drawer and slams the drawer shut.*) What are you doing home?

GUY: I took the night off, if that's all right with you. I was worried about you.

MIRIAM: That's a switch.

GUY: Where have you been?

MIRIAM: I went to see "My Fair Lady."

GUY: We were supposed to see that on Sunday.

MIRIAM: I saw it tonight.

GUY: You know how I hate to go to the movies by myself.

MIRIAM: You can go with Kenny.

GUY: Kenny is gone for the week-end.

MIRIAM: All right, I'll go again.

GUY: We were supposed to economize.

MIRIAM: Then I won't go again.

GUY: Did you like it?

MIRIAM: Yes. I loved it. A little overblown and a little too long, but yes, it was lovely.

GUY: You're angry with me.

MIRIAM: Why in the world should I be angry with you?

GUY: I forgot to call.

MIRIAM: Did you really?

GUY: In all the excitement I just plumb forgot.

MIRIAM: What excitement was that?

GUY: Those kids are unbelievable. They did a scene in class from "Awake and Sing." It nearly blew my mind.

MIRIAM: How did it go?

GUY: What?

MIRIAM: The audition. How did it go? You did go, didn't you?

GUY: Yes. Yes, I went.

MIRIAM: And? How did it go? Watch my lips—.

GUY: All right.

MIRIAM: Did you read?

GUY: Yes. I read.

MIRIAM: And? What did they say?

GUY: Thank you.

MIRIAM: You don't want to talk about it.

GUY: I don't want to talk about it because you're really not interested. Well, if you really must know it was an absolute nightmare. Not really, no. It's just that it's been so long—. When I first got there

there was no one in sight, absolutely no one. Except, of course, for a couple of actors just sitting around and waiting. So, I took off my coat, sat down and waited. Do you remember Ted Carter? A roly-poly little man—not much of an actor, but a very sweet guy. And Henry Curtis. Tall, dark, thin. He was in Myron's class. Of course, he's now slightly grey—. Anyway there they were—faces from the dear dead past—and they welcomed me with open arms. You know, my dear, there's a world out there I'd forgotten ever existed. They were so bright, so cheerful, so optimistic and I said to myself, "How do they go on like this? Year after year? How do they earn a living?"

MIRIAM: They drive a cab.

GUY: I'm talking about people that never got anywhere, people that never made it. At least if I died tomorrow I could say that I've starred on Broadway. I've played leading roles in the movies. But these men. They keep slogging along. I don't know. Maybe I'm crazy, but I love actors. I think we're a noble lot and I think the theatre is a noble calling. In what other profession does a man lay himself on the line like that? Night after night we stand up on that stage, our souls stripped bare for all the world to see. And for what? To give our fellow man a little pleasure? To shed some small dim light on the human mind? And then, no matter how successful, the show eventually closes and we're out of work; and we start all over again. Maybe that's what keeps us so young. What do you think?

MIRIAM: Don't ask me.

GUY: You're living with one.

MIRIAM: Actors are just a little bit full of themselves.

GUY: In order to survive, my dear, in order to survive. Anyway, the casting director finally introduced herself to me and she ushered me into this room. And there they were—all in a row—behind this long table. And there was this deadly silence. Finally one of them said, "What have you done lately?" I said, "King Lear." I think that may have confused them. I'm sure they thought King Lear was some sort of a beer. And then this sweet lady pipes up and says, "Would you mind telling us your age, Mr. Leonard?"

MIRIAM: And what did you say?

GUY: I said that I would. And then Jerry asked me if I'd mind reading some copy and I said that I'd be happy to and I read one of the spots and then someone said would I mind reading something else and I said that I'd be happy to oblige and I read a second spot, and then someone said, "Thank you" and I was ushered out.

MIRIAM: And that was it?

GUY: Actually the casting director was really very nice. She apologized for all the confusion and she offered to put me in touch with a couple of agents and she suggested that I get some pictures, a resume and an answering service.

MIRIAM: An answering service?

GUY: To answer the phone when no one was in! Then Jerry came out of the room and he walked down the hall with me. He told me to leave my clothing sizes with the receptionist and he said that he'd be in touch with me this evening. I said that I'd be out, that Friday was one of my best nights. I told him that you would be in and that I would be in touch with you.

MIRIAM: I went out to mail Karen's birth certificate.

GUY: She doesn't leave until the Spring.

MIRIAM: It does take a while to get a passport.

GUY: Seven years, as I recall.

MIRIAM: Anyway on the way home I passed the theatre and the timing was right and I needed some cheering up so I went in. I left your dinner in the oven. Did you find it? I feel like I'm talking to the wall.

GUY: What?

MIRIAM: Your—dinner—in—the—oven. Did—you—find—it?

GUY: No.

MIRIAM: I always leave it in the oven, you know that.

GUY: I ate out.

MIRIAM: Where did you eat?

GUY: I ate at Sardi's, my dear.

MIRIAM: Sardi's?

GUY: That's right. Sardi's. After the audition I was walking down Madison Avenue and I said to myself, "The hell with it! I need a drink!" So I strolled over to Sardi's. And guess who I met there.

MIRIAM: Elizabeth Taylor.

GUY: Try Betty Gardner. I'm standing at the bar when who should walk in the door but—.

MIRIAM: Betty Gardner.

GUY: "My God!" she screamed, the way Betty does. —You could hear her on 42nd Street—and we fell all over one another.

MIRIAM: What was Betty doing in Sardi's?

GUY: She was there to celebrate.

MIRIAM: Celebrate what?

GUY: Her first movie in over ten years. And guess what kind of a movie she's in. A horror film. Can you see Betty in a horror film?

(MIRIAM shakes her head.)

GUY: Well, that's what she's doing. A horror film. She plays a spinster librarian. She is one of the last to go, however. First she gets stabbed to death. Then she gets chopped up with a meat cleaver and then piece by piece she gets fed into this cement mixer.

MIRIAM: How did she get the job? Watch my lips.

GUY: She got a call from this producer out on the Coast. When she first knew him he was an assistant to an assistant A.D. A "gofer." Now he's a big producer. Well, a producer, at any rate.

MIRIAM: Of horror films.

GUY: What can I tell you? They're flying her out to the Coast. Paying all her expenses. Putting her up in a fancy hotel and she gets four weeks work. While she's out there she's going to contact several agents.

MIRIAM: What about Harry?

GUY: He's selling insurance now.

MIRIAM: I know all that. Are they still together?

GUY: As far as I know.

MIRIAM: They pilloried that man.

GUY: Ralph Johnson is doing a TV show for CBS, by the way. And guess what the subject is. It's about blacklisting. So—maybe the dark days are over. What do you think?

MIRIAM: I think that Sardi's is very expensive.

GUY: Betty paid. She insisted on it. As a matter of fact, we had a big fight about the check. We finally ended up tossing for it—and I lost.

MIRIAM: Thank God!

(The telephone rings.)

GUY: That might be Jerry.

MIRIAM: You want me to answer it.

GUY: You live here, don't you?

MIRIAM: If it's for you—.

GUY: I said I wouldn't be home. And I don't want him to think that I'm just sitting around waiting for his call.

MIRIAM: What do you want me to say?

GUY: If it's Jerry just take the message.

MIRIAM: (*SHE picks up the phone.*) Hello? Yes. Yes, I'm home. Yes. Yes, he is. If you insist. (*SHE hangs up.*)

GUY: What was that all about? Was it Jerry?

MIRIAM: No, it was George.

GUY: George Makapoulos??

MIRIAM: No, George Raft. He was calling from the phone on the corner. He's coming up.

GUY: Why did you tell him that I was here?

MIRIAM: Because I'm not gonna lie for you anymore.

GUY: When did you ever lie for me?

MIRIAM: I've spent my life lying for you.

GUY: I won't see him.

MIRIAM: You're afraid to see him, aren't you.

GUY: Don't be ridiculous. I have nothing to say to the man.

MIRIAM: Apparently he has something to say to you.

GUY: He can say it to you. Since you're the one that's so anxious to see him.

MIRIAM: What are you gonna do?

GUY: I'm going to bed.

MIRIAM: At this hour?

GUY: I've had a long day. I need all the sleep I can get.

(The intercom buzzer rings. MIRIAM answers it.)

MIRIAM: Yes?

DOORMAN's VOICE: Mr. Makapoulos.

MIRIAM: Send him up. (*SHE turns to GUY.*) Good night.

GUY: You're actually gonna sit and talk to that man.

MIRIAM: I'm not gonna throw him out.

GUY: You sure have changed your tune.

MIRIAM: Guy, you can't hold a grudge forever.

GUY: A grudge? Is that what you call it? A grudge? That man is a monster. He is unspeakable.

MIRIAM: What else is new?

GUY: Does he actually expect me to forgive and forget? Is that what he expects? He must be out of his mind. Well, that's one thing I'll say for him. He hasn't lost his nerve.

MIRIAM: Chutzpah.

GUY: What? Yes. Yes, chutzpah. That's what it takes, you know. The ability to step on people. I never had it. That's why I'm driving a cab today. I'm not gonna hide. If that son of a bitch has the nerve to show his face, then I'm not gonna hide. He's the one that ought to hide. I'm just afraid—.

MIRIAM: What? I'll hide all the knives.

GUY: It's no joking matter. You know what a temper I have.

MIRIAM: You have a temper? That comes a a big surprise.

(The doorbell rings.)

GUY: I hope you don't expect me to answer that door.

(MIRIAM sighs and goes off slowly.)

GEORGE: (*Offstage*) Miriam, my love.

MIRIAM: (*Offstage*) Save it.

GEORGE: (*Offstage*) What's the weather like in there?

MIRIAM: (*Offstage*) Go in and find out.

(GEORGE MAKAPOULOS, a slim, dark, intense looking man around fifty, enters. HE is holding a large manila envelope. The TWO MEN stand looking at one another.)

GEORGE: These are the rewrites. (*HE tosses the envelope onto an end table.*)

GUY: That's what you have to say to me? "These are the rewrites."?

GEORGE: Well, actually, it's the entire script. Revised.

GUY: What script is that?

(MIRIAM enters. GEORGE looks inquiringly at her.)

MIRIAM: Don't look at me. I have some things to do.

GUY: Where are you going? You let this man into my house. Our house—.

MIRIAM: He came to see you.

GEORGE: I'm always happy to see you, my dear.

MIRIAM: Bullshit.

GEORGE: You're a lucky man, Guy. A very lucky man. Why are we standing?

GUY: Because you haven't been invited to sit. Apparently you're here to deliver a script. Thank you.

GEORGE: I'm a "Greek bearing gifts."

GUY: "Beware."

GEORGE: Okay, let's have it.

GUY: Tell me something. In all honesty. In your wildest dreams. Can you actually see us working together again?

GEORGE: I'm a man of vision. In my world anything is possible.

GUY: You're a man of what?

GEORGE: I'm a rat. I'm a traitor. What else? The lowest of the low. Come on, Guy. That's your cue.

GUY: You think this is a joke? You think you can laugh away the death of your friends? You think you can laugh away human debris?

GEORGE: All right. All right. You've got a right to be bitter.

GUY: Thank you. That's very big of you.

GEORGE: (To MIRIAM) May I have a drink?

MIRIAM: I thought you didn't drink.

GEORGE: On occasions, I do. And this is one of them.

MIRIAM: What would you like?

GEORGE: Anything.

MIRIAM: Scotch?

GEORGE: That'll be fine. (*HE sits.*) This is still a great apartment. Very wise investment. What are you thinking, Guy? That you'd like to beat me up? That you'd like to kill me? You're an open book.

(MIRIAM hands him a drink.)

GEORGE: Thank you.

(HE takes a sip of his drink.)

GEORGE: It's strange, isn't it? The twists of fate. If only we knew what life had in store for us. Sit down, Miriam. Please.

(MIRIAM sits. GUY sits)

GUY: If you have something to say, say it.

GEORGE: I did not come here to apologize, if that's what you think. I did not come here to ask your forgiveness. You've lost a great deal, Guy. I am aware of that. But what you've lost you can regain.

GUY: And what have you lost?

GEORGE: I've lost my honor. I've lost my good name.

GUY: Your self respect?

GEORGE: If I'd lost that, I wouldn't be directing this play. I'm gonna talk about this just once, and I will never, ever broach this subject again. I've gone through this with Alfred, and now with you. Why are Americans so smug? So self righteous? Do you really know yourself, Guy? Do you really know what you're made of? I have questioned my motives over the years—.

GUY: And what have you come up with?

GEORGE: I'm still questioning them.

GUY: How convenient.

GEORGE: "What a piece of work is man! How noble in reason! How infinite in faculties!"

GUY: You're going in for Shakespeare now.

GEORGE: I've always loved Shakespeare. It's not my kind of theatre, but I enjoy reading him. I used to think that you and I were in the same boat—both victims of that terrible time. But we're not, you know. You're a hero, Guy. A saint. And I am the devil. That's how I'll go down in history, at any rate. But I don't care. I don't care anymore. I used to eat my heart out. People turned away from me in disgust. I'd open a letter—that said unspeakable things. That threatened my life, but I don't care anymore. I'm still alive and I will not be buried—not until I'm dead. Not you, not anyone is going to do that to me. Hate me, if you want to. That's your privilege, but I'll tell you something, Guy. That hate will do you more harm than me. I've learned to live with the verdict.

GUY: What verdict is that?

GEORGE: That, as far as my so-called friends are concerned, I am a traitor. A Benedict Arnold. Not only my friends, but all the so-called pure in heart. The idealists. All those knights in shining armor with principles that have never had to step down from their high horse and get their little toes wet.

MIRIAM: You're just as eloquent as ever.

GEORGE: You've never liked me, Miriam.

MIRIAM: That's neither here nor there.

GEORGE: Let me put one myth to rest. That picture deal I had with Universal, that was signed long before I went up before that committee. Did I name names to save my own skin? That may have been one of the reasons. I'm quite willing to admit that unashamedly. A drowning man will grab at straws. But that was not the only reason. And it was certainly not the main reason.

GUY: You've got to believe that, don't you?

GEORGE: "Would God the giftie gie us, to see ourselves as others see us."

MIRIAM: You're just full of great literature today.

GEORGE: I'm a frustrated writer. You know that. Well, Guy knows that.

GUY: I don't know you. I thought I did, but I don't know you at all. We are strangers.

GEORGE: That's what my wife keeps telling me. And I'm beginning to think that's true—of all of us. We don't know ourselves, ever. How can we possibly know someone else?

MIRIAM: Still playing the field?

GEORGE: That's none of your business—and if Guy was ever unfaithful—I'm not saying that he was—but if he ever was, it was certainly not my doing.

GUY: You're doing great. You're batting one hundred percent.

GEORGE: Your wife was the one that started this.

MIRIAM: I think I better leave you two alone.

GEORGE: Suit yourself.

(MIRIAM goes off to the bedroom.)

GUY: You would save us both a lot of embarrassment if you left right now. What are you smiling at?

GEORGE: Self righteous people are very unattractive, Guy. Very unattractive.

GUY: I am trying very hard to control myself.

GEORGE: I've noticed that.

GUY: Talk about smug. You oughta be strung up by the balls.

GEORGE: It must feel good to be on the side of the angels. I didn't come here to be insulted.

GUY: What did you come here for?

GEORGE: I'll tell you, if I'm given a chance. For one thing I came here in the hope that you hadn't gone completely sour on life. In the hope that there's some glimmer of objectivity left in what used to be a pretty decent mind. I hurt people and I'm sorry about that. But I'm not sorry about what I did. I did what I thought was right.

GUY: I'm not convinced.

GEORGE: That's your problem, not mine. I love this country. This country is the greatest country in the world. I'm an American because I chose to be. Not because I was born here.

GUY: "I pledge allegiance—"

GEORGE: That's right. I'm a patriot. I have always been a patriot. When I was a communist it was because I thought communism was right for this country, and when I left the party I left it because I thought that communism wasn't good for this country. It's as simple as that. I'm not ashamed of what I am. I'm not ashamed of what I've been. I'm not ashamed of what I've done. And if you can't live with that, tough titty. I want you for this show. Alfred wants you for this show, and the producers want you for this show. And you need us just as much as we need you. That committee was for shit. But I was not gonna lie to them. I have always believed—.

GUY: That honesty is the best policy.

GEORGE: If it's any consolation to you, I am scarred for life.

GUY: The mark of Cain.

GEORGE: So be it. The mark of Cain. But Christ on the cross said, "Forgive them, Father, for they know not what they do."

GUY: All in one evening we get Shakespeare, Robert Burns and the Bible.

GEORGE: You goddamned son of a bitch, you can go straight to hell. (*HE starts off, then turns and faces GUY.*) I have always, always tried to be honest. Truth is what I value in life. Truth above all. You of all people know that much about me. I haven't changed one bit, not as far as that is concerned. And I pray to God I never will. You have the revised script. You can read it or not, as you please. You've got until Sunday. I will call you then. If you're not interested, we'll get someone else. All I can say is, you're a fool if you turn it down.

(GEORGE goes off, GUY sits lost in thought. MIRIAM enters and stands looking from GUY to the doorway.)

END OF ACT I

ACT II

Scene 1

(The action is continuous. GUY is seated. MIRIAM stands watching him. The intercom buzzer is heard. GUY turns and sees MIRIAM.)

GUY: Are you expecting anyone?

MIRIAM: No. (*SHE answers the intercom.*) Yes?

DOORMAN'S VOICE: Mr. Jerry Miller?

MIRIAM: Send him up. (*SHE returns to the living room.*) It's Jerry. Do you want to see him?

GUY: Of course, I want to see him. Why wouldn't I want to see him?

MIRIAM: I don't know, Guy. I really don't know. He's come to offer you the job.

GUY: Now how would you know that?

MIRIAM: Why else would he be here?

GUY: First of all, if I were being offered the job it would be by the casting director. She said she'd be in touch with me this week-end, one way or another.

MIRIAM: Then why is Jerry here?

GUY: To let me down easy.

MIRIAM: Suppose you're offered the job? Guy?

GUY: What?

MIRIAM: I said, suppose you're offered the job—?

GUY: I'll worry about it then.

MIRIAM: In other words, you're considering it.

GUY: I've often considered murder, but I've never committed it.

(The doorbell rings.)

GUY: (*Snapping out.*) Are you gonna answer the door, or aren't you?

MIRIAM: You know something, my dear? I, too, often consider murder. Don't apologize.

GUY: I'm sorry. I'm on edge. If you insist, I will open the door.

MIRIAM: Oh no, no. Please! I wouldn't want you to exert yourself. After all, a dinner at Sardi's can be very exhausting. (*SHE goes off.*) Hello, Jerry. Come on in. Here, I'll take your coat. Go on in.

(Jerry enters. HE seems surprised to see GUY.)

JERRY: Hi.

GUY: I took the night off. Sit down, sit down. Can I get you a drink?

(MIRIAM re-enters.)

GUY: Would you like a drink?

MIRIAM: Not right now, thank you.

JERRY: I'm sorry to barge in on you like this.

GUY: That's quite all right. What'll you have?

JERRY: Do you have any brandy?

GUY: B and B?

JERRY: That'll be fine. I called earlier and there was no one in.

GUY: We went to the movies. That is, the little woman did.

MIRIAM: What little woman?

GUY: My wife. My gorgeous wife went to see "My Fair Lady."

JERRY: Anyway, I thought I'd take a chance. You did say Miriam would be home to take any messages.

MIRIAM: If no one has any objection, Miriam is going to take a shower.

GUY: Good idea.

MIRIAM: *(SHE gives GUY a look.)* I'll see you later, Jerry. *(SHE goes off.)*

JERRY: I hope I'm not interrupting anything.

GUY: No, no, no. *(HE hands Jerry a drink.)*

JERRY: Thank you. Are you joining me?

GUY: I think it's rude to let someone drink alone. *(HE pours himself a healthy Scotch.)* To Cotton Soft.

(THEY drink.)

GUY: Jerry, I—. JERRY: I'm sorry about—.

JERRY: I'm sorry.

GUY: No, no, no. What were you gonna say?

JERRY: I was just gonna say that I was sorry about the mix-up this afternoon. I told them to send you in as soon as you arrived.

GUY: That's quite all right. I ran into some old colleagues of mine and we started to reminisce.

JERRY: That was an excellent reading you gave.

GUY: Thank you. That material was fun to work with.

JERRY: Thank you.

GUY: Jerry, I— JERRY: Guy, I—.

JERRY: I'm sorry.

GUY: That's all right.

JERRY: I was just gonna say that when I spoke to you this afternoon I may have misled you.

GUY: In what way?

JERRY: As I told you, Guy, I have nothing to do with the hiring end of it—.

GUY: I understand.

JERRY: That fact of the matter is, I mentioned forty thousand dollars as the session fee. Connie hasn't called you, by the way. Has she?

GUY: No.

JERRY: Well, that's what they were offering Jason Potts, you see.

GUY: As a matter of fact, I'm glad you stopped by. I was gonna give you a ring.

(The telephone rings.)

JERRY: Isn't that your phone?

GUY: What's that? Yes. Yes, I think it is. (*HE stands up and looks offstage.*) Miriam? (*HE turns to JERRY.*) I guess I better answer it. (*HE goes into the breakfast room and picks up the phone.*) Hello? This is he. Oh, hello, Connie. Fine. Just fine. I see. Well, Connie—. I see. Well—. I see. Well, Connie—. I see. Right. Right. Right. I see. Thank you. Good-bye Connie. (*HE hangs up, stands looking slightly confused, then wanders back into the living room.*) Yes. Well, I guess I've been booked.

JERRY: That's great! Congratulations.

GUY: Thank you. They're paying thirty thousand dollars. For the first two spots, that is, and I'll be signing an exclusive contract—for commercials, that is, with Cotton Soft.

JERRY: That's wonderful, Guy.

GUY: It's been quite some time since I've been in front of a camera.

JERRY: I'm sure it'll all come back to you. Your glass is empty.

GUY: Please, help yourself.

JERRY: Thank you. (*HE pours himself a drink and sips it.*) I'm so glad it all worked out. I'm really looking forward to this. It may not be a feature film, but we are conscientious. As a matter of fact, I was working on this thirty second spot last week, for a local bank. We started at four in the afternoon and didn't wind up till four the next morning.

GUY: Oh?

JERRY: Yes, well, it did go on for quite a bit, but you must remember we're under a lot of pressure. Millions of dollars, you see, riding on this one little spot. We lose one account—like Coca Cola—for example, or Edgewood and heads begin to roll—and I mean like two, three hundred people at a time.

GUY: I see.

JERRY: I've got a couple of spots running now that I'm sort of proud of. There's one for Jupiter Cleanser, where this young couple meet in the laundry room. And then there's the one for Tasty Margarine, where the old lady bakes all those pies and they disappear one by one. That's one of mine. You must have seen that one.

GUY: Yes, I think I have.

JERRY: I did toy once with the idea of becoming an actor. That was after I saw you in "The Day of Judgement." I said to myself, "Wow! If I could do that to an audience!"

GUY: But you never followed through.

JERRY: Not really, no. But I do get to read with the actors every once in a while. At auditions, I mean. (*HE pauses, then continues, rather tentatively.*) I guess it must have been pretty rough on you.

GUY: What's that.

JERRY: I mean all those years. You were doing so well, and then suddenly—nothing.

GUY: I'll tell you something, Jerry. I think, sometimes, that things work out for the best. Take the holocaust, for example. If not for the holocaust I doubt if there'd be a state of Israel now.

JERRY: Quite possibly.

GUY: It's true. Before that committee came along I was going great guns. I could pick and choose and the money was rolling in. My personal life, however, was a mess. As a matter of fact, Mimi was ready to throw in the towel and—looking back—I really can't blame her. And then suddenly the whole world collapsed around us and we clung to each other. We clung to each other for dear life. Back at Ohio State I played the Duke in "As You Like It." The good duke, that is. He has this speech. "Sweet are the uses of adversity/ Which like the toad, ugly and venomous/ Wears yet a precious jewel in his head/ And this our life, exempt form public haunt/ Finds tongues in trees, books in the running brooks/ Sermons in stones and good in everything." And I'm putting you to sleep.

JERRY: What's that? I'm sorry.

GUY: It's been a long day.

JERRY: And one too many martinis.

GUY: I'll drive you home. I've got my cab nearby.

JERRY: No, no, no. I'll be all right.

GUY: How about joining us for dinner?

JERRY: Well—.

GUY: I take Sunday off. Unless you've made other plans.

JERRY: Well, no. Not exactly.

GUY: Good. Let me check with Miriam. I'm sure it's all right. Our son's away for the week-end and I'm sure she'll be glad to have you. (*HE goes toward the hallway.*) Miriam? Miriam?

(MIRIAM enters in a housecoat.)

GUY: I've asked Jerry to join us for dinner on Sunday.

JERRY: You may have made other plans.

MIRIAM: We'd love to have you.

JERRY: I don't want to impose.

MIRIAM: We would love to have you. As a matter of fact, why don't you bring your girlfriend? We'd like to meet her. Wouldn't we, Guy?

GUY: Yes. Yes, of course.

JERRY: Janet's out of town for the week-end. She's visiting her brother upstate.

MIRIAM: You're all alone then. That'll work out perfectly.

JERRY: I'll bring the wine. Do you know what you'll be having?

GUY and MIRIAM: Chicken.

JERRY: I know just the thing.

MIRIAM: Yes, I've heard that you're quite an expert when it comes to alcoholic beverages. What are you looking for?

JERRY: My attache case. Whoops! (*HE clings to the chair to prevent himself from falling.*)

MIRIAM: Are you all right?

JERRY: I must have left it in the office—I'd better be going.

MIRIAM: It's this way, Jerry.

JERRY: Right. Right. See you on Sunday, then. (*HE shakes hands with GUY.*)

MIRIAM: We eat around three o'clock. Is that all right? It's this way, Jerry.

JERRY: Right.

(MIRIAM leads JERRY off to the foyer. GUY sits lost in thought.)

MIRIAM: (*Offstage.*) Straight down the hall.

(GUY picks up his glass, sees that it's empty and sets it down again. MIRIAM re-enters.)

MIRIAM: How did he take it?

GUY: What's that?

MIRIAM: You did turn him down, didn't you? Oh, Guy!

GUY: He has his heart set on my doing this commercial.

MIRIAM: After all your preaching.

GUY: Well I'm certainly not gonna make a career of it. As a matter of fact—.

MIRIAM: As a matter of fact what?

GUY: I'll be signing an exclusive contract with Cotton Soft. And that will be the extent of my commercial career.

MIRIAM: For how long?

GUY: What do you mean?

MIRIAM: How long is the contract for?

GUY: Two years, I think. It's just a stepping stone.

MIRIAM: Stepping stone to what?

GUY: To getting me back on my feet again. I'll be appearing on all the major networks. Do you know what that means? NBC. CBS. ABC. I'll be kosher again. You know what that means, don't you? Kosher again?

MIRIAM: Yes, my dear. I know what that means.

GUY: I'll be coming into all those people's homes. All those directors and producers. All those men who didn't have the guts to hire me. The Ernie Buttrams and the Dick Wendells. Besides, we need the money. Remember? And do you know how much I stand to make? Thirty thousand dollars. To begin with, that is. Thirty thousand dollars. And that's just a drop in the bucket.

MIRIAM: You could do Alfred's play.

GUY: I will never do Alfred's play, never! Not as long as George Makapoulos is directing it.

MIRIAM: If Alfred made it up with him—.

GUY: I've lost my respect for Alfred as well. You know why that son of a bitch came here. He came here because he needs me now. And where was he when I needed him? All he had to do was to pick up the phone. "Is there anything I can do for you, Guy? Do you need any money, Guy?" You mean to tell me he couldn't have said something to someone? Put in a good word for me.

MIRIAM: And if he had called you up, would you have spoken to him?

GUY: That is not the point. He could have made the effort. He should have made the effort. That's what I would have done. That's what you would have done. That's what any decent human being would have done.

MIRIAM: It's not as if you'd have to socialize with him.

GUY: You don't understand. You have never understood. The relationship between an actor and a director—it's like a marriage. How could I possibly work with a man that turns my stomach! That fucking slime! That murderer! And he's proud of what he's done.

MIRIAM: I don't think—.

GUY: That's right. You don't think. Didn't you hear what he said? That man ruined my life. He ruined my life. I couldn't work here, I couldn't leave the country. I had two jobs in England. They were just waiting for me. You remember that? I could have had a fantastic career—doing all the classics.

MIRIAM: You were never right for Hamlet.

GUY: Neither was Richard Burbage. I just hope that our daughter doesn't have to go through what we went through.

MIRIAM: What do you mean?

GUY: She wants to go to England, doesn't she? She is our daughter, isn't she. She has my name, doesn't she?

MIRIAM: You mean our passports? We got them eventually.

GUY: Eventually. Seven years too late. Have you forgotten? Have you forgotten what it was like? Hounded by the F.B.I. Ostracized by our neighbors. (*HE grabs her by the wrist and drags her into the breakfast room.*) I'd like to read you something.

MIRIAM: Guy, you're hurting me.

GUY: (*HE pushes her into a chair, then takes the box of letters from the drawer and rummages through them.* Where's that letter? Ah, here we are. (*HE reads sections of the letter, growing more heated as HE proceeds.*) "Miss Dorothy Dayton, Passport Office. Department of State. Washington, D.C.—"Dear Miss Dayton—." This was after that Supreme Court decision. "The right to travel is a part of the liberty of which the citizen cannot be deprived . . ." Ah! Here we are. "There is a considerable group of artists who have been deprived by our government of the right to professional employment. They may not act, dance, sing, play, direct, or write for motion pictures or for television." (*HE tosses the letter aside and picks up another.*)

MIRIAM: Guy, please! I wrote those letters.

GUY: May twenty-ninth, nineteen fifty-four. Beverly Hills. That was before we were forced to sell our home. Before we were forced to flee. Before we were forced to run for our lives.

MIRIAM: Guy—.

GUY: (*HE reads.*) "Dear Mr. Wilcox, as principal of the school that our young son, Kenny attends, as an authority in the field of education, as a pillar of this respectable community, we feel that you're the proper person to turn to."

(*MIRIAM starts to rise.*)

GUY: You sit down and listen! (*HE continues to read, sometimes not even referring to the letter, he knows it so well.*) "Last month my wife drove my daughter, Karen, to a rehearsal of the school play, sponsored by the PTA. Suddenly it appeared that my wife had become invisible. All the women that she thought were her friends, or at least friendly ac-quaintances, all those women turned their backs on her and looked the other way. Among the ladies who took part in this barbaric ritual, I am sad to say, was your own wife." (*HE turns to MIRIAM.*) Do you remember that?

MIRIAM: Yes, my dear. I remember.

GUY: (*Reading.*) "Petitions have been circulated in our neighborhood trying to force us to sell our house. We've received threatening notes in the mail—one of them decorated with human feces. Rocks have been hurled at our windows and bodies of dead animals, together with buckets of filth have been left on our doorstep."

MIRIAM: Guy, please.

GUY: Shut up and listen! (*HE reads.*) "Two weeks ago, as I was returning home from a nearby restaurant, I was attacked by three young men. As a result of this beating I now sport three broken ribs, plus other more visible evidence of this brutal assault."

MIRIAM: How long can we go on brooding about this?

GUY: (*Reading.*) "At the beginning of this school term we entrusted to your care our young son, Kenny, a pleasant, good humored boy, who enjoyed all sorts of extra curricular activity, and especially the friendship of his classmates. During the course of attending your school our son has been made the object of ridicule and of scorn. He's been encouraged to deny his own parents. His one remaining friend has been labeled a traitor to his country, because he associated with our son."

(MIRIAM starts to rise.)

GUY: I'm not finished yet. (*Reading.*) "We're speaking here of a ten year old boy. Our son is now a care-worn neurotic child who begs us not to send him back to your custody." (*HE tosses the letter onto the table in front of her.*) And you want me to forget? Forget? As long as I live I shall never forget. Where are you going?

MIRIAM: I'm going to bed. I'm tired.

GUY: You have nothing to say? No words of wisdom?

MIRIAM: No, my dear. Not when you get like this. (*SHE kisses him.*) Don't forget to turn off the light. (*SHE goes off to the bedroom.*)

GUY: (*Calling after her.*) The light is out, in case you haven't noticed! The light's been out for the past twelve years!

(HE sits and studies the letter, then tosses it back into the box. HE wanders into the living room, picks up the empty glass, sets it down again, takes a fresh glass, pours a healthy drink of Scotch and takes a swig. HE starts for a chair, returns for the bottle and settles into the chair with the bottle on the floor beside him. HE rests his head on the back of the chair, and HE sings softly.)

GUY: "Oh, the moon shone bright on pretty Red Wing, As she lay sleeping, a treasure keeping—."

(The lights come down.)

END OF ACT II, Scene 1

ACT II

Scene 2

Early afternoon the following Sunday. The telephone rings. MIRIAM, an apron over her dress, enters the breakfast room from the kitchen and picks up the phone.

MIRIAM: Hello? Yes, George, what is it? He isn't in right now. He went out to do some shopping. He should be back very shortly. We'll be in all afternoon. Right. (*SHE hangs up, sighs, looks about then opens a drawer and takes out a table cloth, which SHE throws over the table. SHE sees a hole in the cloth.*) Damn! (*SHE sighs, removes the tablecloth, tosses it onto a chair, takes another one from the drawer, inspects it carefully and tosses it over the table. SHE takes out napkins from the drawer that match the first cloth, sighs, hesitates then finally tosses them onto the table. SHE searches the drawer again.*) Damn! Damn, damn, damn, damn, damn! (*SHE slams the drawer shut and then stands listening.*) Guy? Guy? (*MIRIAM picks up the damaged cloth and goes off to the kitchen.*)

(GUY enters from the foyer with a bag of groceries, which HE sets on the table.)

MIRIAM: (*Offstage.*) Guy?

GUY: No, it's Rex Harrison.

MIRIAM: (*Re-enters.*) What took you so long?

GUY: This is supposed to be a day of rest. Where do all those people come from? Did Karen call?

MIRIAM: No. Not yet. And when she does call, please, for heaven sakes, will you please not nag at her.

GUY: I think I have a right to ask my little girl where she's been.

MIRIAM: Your little girl is a sophomore at Northwestern. She's twenty years old and she's entitled to a certain amount of privacy.

GUY: Why? You think she has something to hide?

MIRIAM: Oh, for God sakes! (*SHE looks through the groceries.*) Where is the cheese?

GUY: What cheese?

MIRIAM: The cheese I put on the list.

GUY: There was no cheese—.

MIRIAM: Okay, okay.

GUY: There was—.

MIRIAM: (*Angrily.*) I said okay. Will you please forget it!! It is not important.

GUY: Then why are you so hysterical?

MIRIAM: I am not hysterical!

GUY: You'd think I'd stolen the eternal light from your synagogue.

(SHE sighs impatiently.)

GUY: Your tone was accusatory.

MIRIAM: There is no such word!

(HE strides into the living room.)

MIRIAM: I take it back.

(GUY returns with the dictionary.)

MIRIAM: I take it back. There is such a word.

GUY: Then why did you say there wasn't?

MIRIAM: Because you are slowly driving me out of my mind.

GUY: (*Reading.*) "Accusatory: containing or expressing accusation." Where is the list?

MIRIAM: What?

GUY: The grocery list. Where did you put it?

MIRIAM: I gave it to you.

GUY: I put it in the bag.

MIRIAM: It is not in the bag. Look for yourself.

(HE looks in the bag and then starts for the living room.)

MIRIAM: (*Furiously.*) Oh, Jesus Christ!

GUY: (*HE stops in his tracks.*) And please don't use our Lord's name in vain.

MIRIAM: He is not my lord.

GUY: Is that any reason to be disrespectful?

MIRIAM: Guy, please!

(HE goes off to the foyer. MIRIAM sighs and puts the groceries back into the bag. GUY re-enters waving a piece of paper.)

MIRIAM: What? What? What? Tell me what?

GUY: Where does it say cheese?

(HE hands the list to her. SHE looks at it, turns it over and hands it back to GUY.)

GUY: I don't believe it.

MIRIAM: There was no room on the front.

GUY: There was no room on the front because the paper's so small. I know we are poor, but surely we can afford a piece of scrap paper that's a little bit bigger than my thumb.

MIRIAM: We don't even need the cheese—. (*Biting her tongue.*) Oh, no!

GUY: If we don't need the cheese, why did you put it on the list? I'm asking merely for information.

MIRIAM: I was planning to serve some cheese with the drinks. However I do have some cheese in the refrigerator which I was planning to use for sandwiches in the morning, so the problem is solved.

GUY: You mean that stuff that's been in there for weeks?

MIRIAM: They age cheese for years.

GUY: In our refrigerator? And why must everything in that box be wrapped in tinfoil? It's impossible to tell what's in there.

MIRIAM: Everything is labeled.

GUY: I'm not referring to the freezer.

MIRIAM: Why are you sniffling like that? You were sniffling.

GUY: I don't know. I might be coming down with something.

MIRIAM: What?

GUY: Do I look like a doctor?

MIRIAM: Let me feel your head. Your head's ice cold.

GUY: I've just come in from the cold. It's the middle of January.

MIRIAM: I'll get you some aspirin.

GUY: Aspirins upset my stomach.

MIRIAM: Not if you take them with milk.

GUY: Milk gives me gas. I am fine. I will live.

MIRIAM: Then do me a favor. Go into the living room. The Sunday Times is yours—all yours for a change. And please, will you please put that dictionary back on the shelf!

GUY: What a grouch!

(MIRIAM takes the bag of groceries into the kitchen. GUY takes the dictionary into the living and returns it to its place. HE sits down, picks up a section of the paper, glances at it, then sets it down and re-enters the breakfast room, sitting at the table. MIRIAM re-enters, notices GUY, sighs with annoyance then takes out dishes and starts to set the table.)

GUY: How's the dinner coming? Watch my lips.

MIRIAM: Everything is under control—except for me.

GUY: What's the matter with you?

MIRIAM: I'm a nervous wreck.

GUY: What are you nervous about?

MIRIAM: You know perfectly well what I'm nervous about. I am always nervous when we have guests for dinner.

GUY: There's only one guest and he just happens to be an old friend of yours. And besides, you've been cooking dinners for twenty-five years. You certainly ought to have it down to a system by now.

MIRIAM: You've been acting longer than that and you still throw up on opening night.

GUY: I have never thrown up on opening night. That's Helen Hayes—I think. And besides giving a performance in front of a few thousand people is just a little bit more demanding than cooking a simple dinner.

MIRIAM: Have you ever cooked a simple dinner?

GUY: It's all a matter of timing.

MIRIAM: Why don't you set the table?

GUY: I'd rather watch you. You're very sexy when you're setting a table. What are we having?

MIRIAM: What?

GUY: What are we having for dinner?

MIRIAM: Chicken.

GUY: I know that. What kind of chicken? How did you prepare it?

MIRIAM: Chicken marsala. We're having green beans with almonds, cooked in mushroom soup. We're having sweet potatoes cooked with pineapple and little marshmallows. A salad with French or Italian dressing. Hot biscuits. And for dessert we're having vanilla ice cream topped with your favorite chocolate syrup. Now does that answer your question?

GUY: No soup?

MIRIAM: No soup.

GUY: If we're having such a fancy dinner how come we're eating in here?

MIRIAM: Because there are only three of us and I'm certainly not going to put on airs for Jerry.

(The telephone rings.)

MIRIAM: Will you please answer that!

GUY: Yes, ma'am. (*He picks up the phone.*) Hello? Hey, Princess, I was beginning to worry about you. It is not Sunday morning, it is Sunday afternoon. What time did you get to bed last night?

MIRIAM: Guy, please!

GUY: Your mother says, "Guy, please!" Your mother thinks that I'm a nag. Oh, yeah. Well just you wait. I was gonna say a parent. If you think it's easy being a mother, the wife of a father—.

MIRIAM: You can say that again!

GUY: How are your new classes? The philosophy class is new. Hold on. She wants to speak to you. (*HE hands the phone to MIRIAM.*)

MIRIAM: (*On the phone.*) I mailed it on Friday.

GUY: Ask her if she needs any money.

MIRIAM: (*To GUY.*) If she needs any money she will ask for it.

GUY: Will you please ask her?

MIRIAM: (*On the phone.*) Your father wants to know if you need any money. (*SHE turns to GUY.*) "If I need any money I will ask for it." (*Back on the phone.*) Kenny's been accepted by Harvard. He's spending the week-end with his friend, Tommy. That's our affair. We will manage! All right. Dress warmly. And don't forget to send that snapshot. (*SHE hangs up.*) She's going skating. (*SHE continues to set the table.*) How come you didn't tell her about the commercial? Guy?

GUY: I heard you the first time. I've been thinking. No cracks, please.

MIRIAM: What have you been thinking? Why can't you tell them that you've simply changed your mind?

GUY: It's not as simple as that. At this very moment they're putting my wardrobe together.

MIRIAM: On a Sunday?

GUY: They called me on a Saturday, didn't they? They start shooting the day after tomorrow.

MIRIAM: You mean to tell me that you're the only actor in New York?

GUY: They had someone else and they weren't happy with him.

MIRIAM: Why are you telling me this?

GUY: Who else am I gonna tell it to?

MIRIAM: I don't think Jerry would want you to do this commercial if you felt the least bit uneasy about it.

GUY: Then you think that I should just tell him that I've had second thoughts.

MIRIAM: I couldn't have put it better myself.

GUY: When? When do you think I should tell him? Before we eat? After we eat? After we've had a couple of drinks?

MIRIAM: May I ask you a simple question?

GUY: (*Glumly.*) That all depends.

MIRIAM: I know why you wanted to audition. You wanted to exercise your atrophied muscles. But why, in heaven's name, did you say yes when they offered it to you?

GUY: Because I'm a whore. Is that what you wanted to hear? Whisper in my ear and I am yours. Is that what you wanted to hear?

(The intercom buzzer rings. MIRIAM sighs and answers it.)

MIRIAM: Yes?

DOORMAN'S VOICE: Jerry Miller.

MIRIAM: Send him up.

GUY: It's not easy being a frog.

MIRIAM: I beg your pardon?

GUY: That's the first part I ever played; the part of a frog in a garden.

MIRIAM: Where was that?

GUY: In the second grade. All during the play I had to hop about all crouched over. In the middle of the play I got tired so I stopped. And the teacher said, "What's the matter, Guy? Are you all right?" And I said, "I'm all right, Miss Wyckoff. It's not easy being a frog." And the teacher said—.

MIRIAM: What?

GUY: (*Woefully.*) It's not easy being anything.

MIRIAM: Are you making this up?

GUY: The fact of the matter is I am an actor. I cannot cope with reality. That's why I became an actor.

MIRIAM: Jerry is a very nice boy and I'm sure that he will understand.

GUY: That's all very well but it just so happens that I am committed. I'm committed to Continental. I'm committed to Cotton Soft. And I am ready to be committed!

MIRIAM: Have you signed the contract? Very well then. I may not come from a family of lawyers, but even I know that a verbal agreement isn't legally binding in a court of law.

GUY: That's all I need!

MIRIAM: What?

GUY: A court of law! After all that we've been through!

MIRIAM: (*Remembering.*) Oh, God!

GUY: What now?

MIRIAM: Jerry's bringing wine. I think we may have some wine glasses left. They're on the top shelf. Will you please reach them for me?

GUY: (*HE stands on a chair.*) How many? How many do you need?

MIRIAM: Three. There are three of us! One. Two. Three.

GUY: Okay, okay. Where are you going?

MIRIAM: To rinse them off. They've been on that shelf for years. (*SHE takes the glasses into the kitchen.*)

GUY: They're perfectly clean. (*GUY closes the cabinet door and puts the chair back into place.*)

(*The doorbell rings.*)

MIRIAM: (*Offstage.*) Is that the doorbell?

GUY: (*Ignoring her call.*) That's the doorbell!

MIRIAM: (*Offstage.*) Will you please answer it?

(*GUY sighs, goes into the living room, notices the Sunday Times is spread about and stops to straighten it. MIRIAM re-enters with the wine glasses and places them on the table.*)

MIRIAM: (*SHE studies the table.*) We really should have flowers.

(*The doorbell rings.*)

MIRIAM: Guy?!

GUY: Okay, okay. You're turning into a shrew. Did you know that?

(*GUY goes off to the foyer. MIRIAM removes her apron, checks her hair in the mirror, then straightens the glasses on the table.*)

GUY: (*Offstage.*) Hello, Jerry. Come on in.

(*MIRIAM suddenly remembers something else and dashes off to the kitchen. GUY, holding a bag, enters with JERRY.*)

GUY: Come on in. Mimi? Jerry's here. Sit down, Jerry. Mimi?

(*MIRIAM enters the living room.*)

MIRIAM: Hello, Jerry.

JERRY: Hi. You look particularly ravishing.

MIRIAM: (*To GUY.*) Watch and learn.

GUY: Jerry brought us some wine.

JERRY: It should be kept chilled.

MIRIAM: Thank you dear. We can have it with our dinner.

GUY: I'll put it in the refrigerator. (*HE goes off to the kitchen.*)

MIRIAM: Sit down, Jerry, please.

JERRY: Thank you.

MIRIAM: What's it like outside?

JERRY: It's snowing. Heavily.

MIRIAM: It wasn't supposed to start until tonight. So, how have you been?

JERRY: Just fine.

MIRIAM: I hope you're hungry, because there's lots of food. (*Getting down to business.*) So, tell me about this girl of yours. How long have you been seeing her?

JERRY: I guess it's close to a year now.

MIRIAM: What does she do?

JERRY: She's a teacher.

MIRIAM: What does she teach?

JERRY: Second grade.

MIRIAM: What is she like? Is she pretty? Is she young? Is she old?

JERRY: She's about my age. I think she's pretty and sexy and reasonably intelligent.

MIRIAM: What's wrong with her?

JERRY: You mean, why don't I marry her.

MIRIAM: You said it.

JERRY: Neither of us is interested in marriage.

MIRIAM: Is she Jewish?

JERRY: As a matter of fact, she is.

MIRIAM: Then I find that hard to believe. Okay, okay. I'll mind my own business.

JERRY: Tell me about these kids of yours.

MIRIAM: Well, Karen is a sophomore at Northwestern and captain of her debating team. This Spring she goes to Cambridge—Cambridge, England, that is, to debate the topic of nuclear disarmament.

JERRY: Is she married?

MIRIAM: As a matter of fact, I keep telling her that men are intimidated by intelligent women. (*Slyly.*) Don't you find that so?

JERRY: Give me a dumb broad anytime.

MIRIAM: And Kenny is an Adonis. And he's going to be a brain surgeon. I'm just kidding. He is going to be a doctor though.

JERRY: A Jewish mother's dream.

MIRIAM: And my husband it seems, has gotten himself lost. Guy? (*SHE goes to the breakfast room doorway.*) Guy?

GUY: (*Offstage.*) Coming.

MIRIAM: Have you fallen in? (*Returns to JERRY.*) Would you care for a drink?

JERRY: I've never been known to turn one down.

MIRIAM: I'll let my husband do the honors. Guy?

GUY: (*HE enters with a plastic ice bucket.*) Here we are. All set to go.

MIRIAM: (*In disbelief.*) Where did you get that?

GUY: In the cabinet, under the sink.

MIRIAM: What's wrong with the silver one?

GUY: I forgot all about it. (*To JERRY.*) How about a drink. Scotch? On the rocks?

JERRY: Would a martini be too much trouble? That's all right. Scotch is fine.

GUY: We don't have any vermouth.

JERRY: Scotch is fine.

GUY: How about you?

MIRIAM: Maybe later. Was there something you wanted to discuss with Jerry?

GUY: Right, right. Would you like some ice?

JERRY: I'll take it straight.

GUY: Right. Right. (*He pours a drink and hands it to JERRY.*) Here you are.

JERRY: Thank you. You're not joining me.

GUY: Right. Right.

GUY: I've been thinking, Jerry—. JERRY: Guy, I have some rather—.

JERRY: I'm sorry. What were you gonna say?

GUY: No, no, no. That's quite all right.

JERRY: I'm afraid I have some rather disappointing news. I got a call from Connie last night. It seems as if Cotton Soft has suddenly changed its mind again. They've decided to go along with Jason Potts, after all. I'm sorry, Guy. You'll get your fee, of course.

MIRIAM: Which fee is that?

JERRY: The session fee.

MIRIAM: All of it?

JERRY: Yes, of course. It's a union rule. He was booked. He might have had to turn down another job.

GUY: Whose decision was this? Do you know?

JERRY: Not really, no.

GUY: I don't suppose that Connie had anything to do with it.

JERRY: No! As a matter of fact, Connie's just as upset about all of this as I am. She said to be sure to tell you to call her on Monday. She wants you to meet a couple of agents—if you're interested, that is. I'm sorry, Guy. I feel just awful about it. And I simply cannot understand. They were all so enthusiastic about you. Every last one of them. It's all very confusing.

(The telephone rings.)

MIRIAM: Excuse me. (*SHE goes into the breakfast room and picks up the phone.*) Hello? Yes. Yes, he is. Just a moment, please. (*SHE sets down the receiver and goes into the living room.*) Jerry, it's for you.

JERRY: Oh? Thank you.

MIRIAM: It's right over there.

JERRY: Thank you. (*HE picks up the phone.*) Hello? Oh, hi! How did you get this number? Yes. Yes, of course. I'll get there as soon as I can. No, that's okay. Good-bye. (*HE hangs up and returns to the living room.*) That was Janet. She's visiting her brother, and she missed her train. She has no way of getting back into town. I'm afraid I'm going to have to pick her up.

MIRIAM: You'll have your dinner first. It'll be ready in just a few minutes.

JERRY: I'd love to, but it's a two and a half hour drive and I've got to pick up my car. The roads are very bad up there. And I don't want to drive in the dark, especially in weather like this.

MIRIAM: Yes. Yes, of course.

JERRY: I'm sorry.

MIRIAM: Thank you, Jerry. Thank you for everything.

JERRY: I'm afraid there's not very much to thank me for.

MIRIAM: Forty thousand dollars is nothing to sneeze at. I assume that's what he'll be getting.

JERRY: If that's what was agreed on. I'd better get going. Guy. (*HE shakes hands with GUY.*) I'm terribly sorry.

MIRIAM: We're letting you go on one condition.

JERRY: And what is that?

MIRIAM: The next time you come you bring Janet with you.

JERRY: That's a bargain.

MIRIAM: What about next Sunday?

JERRY: I'll check with Janet and I'll get back to you.

(*MIRIAM goes off with JERRY to the foyer. GUY sits in a daze. HE rises, goes to the liquor cabinet, is about to pour himself a drink then changes his mind and sets the glass down. HE comes downstage looking straight out front, through the window.*)

MIRIAM: (*Offstage.*) Drive carefully. (*SHE re-enters.*) Well? What do you think?

GUY: (*Desolate.*) Isn't it obvious?

MIRIAM: We can't be sure.

GUY: Of course, we can't be sure—since there's no such thing as blacklisting.

MIRIAM: But Betty Gardner. Ralph Johnson. Didn't you say he was doing a show for CBS?

GUY: I knew there was something fishy about all of this. Jerry gave my name to the casting department weeks ago. They could have gotten in touch with me. I'm in the phone book. They could have gotten my number from Jerry.

MIRIAM: The president of Continental is a fan of yours. Jerry said so. Now Guy, we can't be sure.

GUY: (*Ironically.*) That's right, my dear. We can never be sure.

MIRIAM: And besides, we are thirty thousand dollars richer.

GUY: (*Glumly.*) I'll believe it when I see it.

MIRIAM: It's a union rule. Jerry said so. And you're still a member of the union, aren't you?

GUY: By the time they take out taxes—. (*HE sighs.*) I'll never work again. I know it.

MIRIAM: Now, Guy—.

GUY: What's the use of fooling ourselves? (*HE starts to chuckle.*) Do you remember "Li'l Abner"? That cartoon that used to run in the old Daily Mirror?

MIRIAM: What about it?

GUY: There was this character, Bad Luck Joe—. I think that was his name. Anyway everywhere this guy would go there'd be this little dark cloud hanging over him—no matter where he went. No matter what he did—there was always this dark cloud.

MIRIAM: Did Bad Luck Joe make thirty thousand dollars without lifting a finger? Now it's not all black and you know it.

GUY: (*HE smiles sadly.*) "Sermons in stones and good in everything."

MIRIAM: What's that?

GUY: Never mind. Let's eat.

MIRIAM: What's your rush? I haven't even had my drink.

GUY: You're turning into quite a lush these days.

MIRIAM: How about pouring me a drink?

GUY: What is your pleasure?

MIRIAM: We'll get to that later. I think I'll have—some Grand Marnier.

GUY: With or without ice?

MIRIAM: Which do you recommend?

GUY: It's up to you. I think it's a shame to water it down—.

MIRIAM: Then I'll take it straight.

GUY: One Grand Marnier coming up.

MIRIAM: Thank you. Come. Sit beside me.

GUY: You know what that can lead to.

MIRIAM: (*Clarifying.*) I said "sit."

GUY: I don't have my drink.

MIRIAM: If you behave yourself I'll let you have a sip of mine.

(HE settles on the sofa with her.)

MIRIAM: Comfy?

GUY: Mmmmm.

MIRIAM: Guy?

GUY: Yes? What is it?

MIRIAM: George called a little while ago. Calm yourself. I'm only telling you this because he said that he's coming up. Now look if you think I'm anxious for you to take up your career again, you are very much mistaken. Our marriage has never been better. Whenever you're acting, whether it's on the stage or in a movie, you get all wrapped up in the role you're playing.

GUY: That's not always true.

MIRIAM: May I finish, please? The fact of the matter is you're part of another family, a family I have nothing to do with. When you're in a movie you go away on location—for weeks at a time. Sometimes months. Once it was almost a year. I didn't mind it so much because the kids. But now that the kids are gone—or will be soon, n Kenny leaves in the Fall—.

UY: You have your writing.

MIRIAM: You mean that blank piece of paper and that mechanical monster that you call a typewriter?

GUY: Well, apparently you have nothing to worry about.

MIRIAM: But then I think about how miserable it's been for you these past twelve years. Yes, I will have my writing, it's true. But without your work, what will you have now?

GUY: All right. Maybe I could find it in my heart to forgive him—for what he did to me that is. After all, I did become a star under George's direction. What God giveth, God taketh away—and vice versa. But what about the others? The ones beyond recall. The ones that he can never make it up to?

MIRIAM: You mean Myron?

GUY: I mean all the others. I mean Myron and Mary and Jack—just to name a few. Their deaths will haunt me till the end of my days.

MIRIAM: Do you really think that they would have asked this of you? Do you?

GUY: We shall never know, shall we? You don't remember Mary the way she used to be—so bright, so lovely, so full of fun. I keep dreaming about her. I keep seeing her the way she was when we first met, and then I see her the way she was just before she died. Her lovely face all worn and haggard. I keep seeing her in that beat up old fur coat of hers, climbing the steps to that messy, smelly apartment, a bottle of cheap wine clutched to her bosom.

MIRIAM: Mary died of cancer, Guy.

GUY: And Jack—so handsome, so dashing. Women were fighting to go to bed with him. We thought they could never touch him, he was so successful. But they did all right. They stopped him cold.

MIRIAM: Jack had a heart attack. He died "in the saddle," as you so quaintly put it.

GUY: (*Growing more and more obsessive.*) And I keep thinking about Myron. I can't get Myron out of my mind. I keep wondering what was going on in his head. What was he thinking of when he entered that hotel lobby? When he signed that register with a phony name? What was going on in his mind when he rode up that elevator and opened the door to that cold, empty room? And I keep wondering—. Where did he get those pills? Where did they come from? And then I see him sitting on that bed, staring out the window. Staring at the lights of the city coming on slowly, one by one, as the life passed out of him, and I ask myself, "What was going on in his mind?"

MIRIAM: Guy, Sweetie. Listen to me. Myron was a broken man. After Sally died, and then little Jamie, he was never the same.

GUY: Oh, yes, indeed. Myron was a broken man. And George? Where was George? He was out there in Hollywood making one movie after another.

MIRIAM: All right. George made a mistake. He made a mistake! We were living in a time of hysteria. A time when this whole country was in a panic. I'm not particularly fond of George, as you well know. But he is not an evil man. He is not insensitive. He knows how you feel about him and yet he came here. Now that took guts.

GUY: You're telling me?

MIRIAM: He humbled himself by coming here. He humbled himself by calling you and he's coming here again. Do you really think, my dear, that you're in any position to stand in judgment on anyone? Look around you, my love. The world is in a mess. When someone reaches out to you—when someone reaches out to you from the darkness you take his hand.

GUY: You want his hand, you can have it.

MIRIAM: I haven't finished yet. The fact of the matter is I've had it. I've had it up to here. Your sulking, your moping, your self-pity. Either you accept George's offer or I am leaving you.

GUY: Come on, honey—.

MIRIAM: And if you think that I'm not serious, you just try me, my dear. You just try me.

GUY: Come on, Miriam.

MIRIAM: I mean it, Guy. I left you once, remember? This time I won't come back. And now I'm going to start dinner.

(MIRIAM goes into the kitchen. GUY sits lost in thought. Absent-mindedly HE takes a sip of MIRIAM's drink, then sets it down. The intercom buzzes. MIRIAM comes out of the kitchen to answer it.)

MIRIAM: Yes?

DOORMAN'S VOICE: Mr. Makapoulos.

MIRIAM: Send him up. (*SHE goes into the living room.*) That was George. He's coming up. There's a couple of things I think you ought to know. Jenny is dying.

GUY: Who told you that?

MIRIAM: He did. And I don't think even he would lie about a thing like that.

GUY: What else?

MIRIAM: This is the last thing he's going to direct. Alfred's busy writing the screenplay. He'll direct the movie—and according to him, that's it.

GUY: And you believe him.

MIRIAM: I'm telling you what he told me.

(SHE goes into the breakfast room, sighs, looks about and is about to go into the kitchen when the doorbell rings. It rings once. It rings twice. SHE heaves a sigh, goes through the living room, into the foyer.)

MIRIAM: (*Offstage.*) Come in, George.

GEORGE: (*Offstage.*) You have guests.

MIRIAM: (*Offstage.*) The guest is gone. Go on in.

(GEORGE enters. GUY remains seated.)

GEORGE: Don't get up.

(MIRIAM enters. SHE looks at the two of them, goes into the breakfast room and sits down at the table.)

GEORGE: Did you read the rewrites?

GUY: Yes, I read them.

GEORGE: And?

GUY: What's the matter with Jenny?

GEORGE: Miriam told you?

GUY: She said that she's dying. I'm sorry.

GEORGE: Thank you.

GUY: How long?

GEORGE: A few months. At most—a year. But then, who knows?

GUY: Cancer?

(GEORGE nods.)

GUY: What will you do without her?

GEORGE: I didn't come here to discuss my personal life.

GUY: I'm not the least bit interested in your personal life. I happen to be very fond of Jenny.

GEORGE: So am I.

GUY: How she put up with you for all these years. I'm sorry. How can we possibly work together?

GEORGE: I don't know, until we've tried.

GUY: Suppose I quit? Suppose you fire me?

GEORGE: You'll have a run of the play contract.

GUY: You can still fire me.

GEORGE: That's right. And you can still quit.

GUY: You're willing to take a chance? Why? You son of a bitch, why? You need me, don't you? You son of a bitch! You need me badly, don't you.

GEORGE: Don't do this to me, please.

GUY: What? Do what? What am I doing to you?

GEORGE: Even in a war—a victor shows some sort of grace.

GUY: So I'm the victor, am I? Yes, well, maybe I am. Don't you hate me for it?

GEORGE: I don't hate anyone. I never have.

GUY: Well, I'm full of hate.

GEORGE: Yes, I know.

GUY: Can you deal with that? Can you?

GEORGE: Don't do this to me, Guy. Please. Don't do this to me. (*HE weeps.*)

GUY: What an actor! You should be up on that stage. Don't worry, George. I won't tell anyone that you wept. And you know why? Because no one would ever believe me. You'll do anything to get me for this part, wouldn't you?

GEORGE: Anything? No.

GUY: Where do you draw the line?

GEORGE: Let's cut this shit. Do you want to do this play or don't you?

GUY: You know perfectly well that I do.

GEORGE: What does that mean?

GUY: I mean what I say. I'd like to do this play.

GEORGE: Does that mean that you are going to do this play?

GUY: I will, on one condition.

GEORGE: And what condition is that?

GUY: That you're absolutely honest with me.

GEORGE: When have I been otherwise?

GUY: We won't go into that. Miriam told me that you plan to quit directing. Is that true, or isn't it?

GEORGE: It's true.

GUY: Why?

GEORGE: That's my affair. It makes no difference to me whether you believe it or not. I'm being honest with you. That's all you need to know.

GUY: Why did you wait so long? Why did you wait so long to contact me?

GEORGE: We didn't have all the money.

GUY: You expect me to believe that?

GEORGE: It happens to be the truth.

GUY: Are you gonna sit there and tell me that you haven't been talking to other actors?

GEORGE: Alfred wrote that role for you. And just between you and me, I'm not so sure the play can work without you.

GUY: Why are you giving up directing? I want to know. Is it because of Jenny?

GEORGE: No.

GUY: Then why?

GEORGE: Because I'm tired, that's why. I'm tired of being a rug. A rug for everyone to step on. Writers, producers, actors.

GUY: What are you gonna do?

GEORGE: I'm gonna do what I've always wanted to do. I'm gonna write. What are you staring at?

GUY: I'm sorry.

GEORGE: Well, say it.

GUY: What?

GEORGE: Whatever you're thinking. Just say it.

GUY: I was thinking that maybe there is a God after all.

GEORGE: I don't expect us to be friends. Not like we used to be. That's all over with. But I respect you and you respect my talent. Or don't you.

GUY: Yes. Yes, I do.

GEORGE: Then there's nothing more to say. Is there?

GUY: I guess not.

GEORGE: Do you want to talk about the play?

GUY: Not right now.

GEORGE: Alfred and I would like your input. Rehearsals start on Tuesday. Can you have lunch with us on Monday, say around one?

GUY: Where?

GEORGE: Alfred's apartment.

GUY: I'll see you then.

GEORGE: Right. You don't have to shake hands with me.

GUY: You stupid son of a bitch! I'm sorry, I'm sorry.

GEORGE: I expect a rather stormy rehearsal. Alfred, too, gets hysterical at times. All grist for the mill. (*HE calls out.*) Miriam, I assume that you've been listening. I'm leaving now.

(MIRIAM enters the living room.)

GEORGE: God bless us all!

(GEORGE goes off. A moment later a door slam is heard. MIRIAM and GUY embrace. THEY sit on the sofa and GUY rests his head on her bosom. SHE strokes his head. HE begins to weep.)

MIRIAM: Shhh. Shhh.

CURTAIN

SHAKESPEARE REVISITED

A Miniplay

CAST OF CHARACTERS

Joanne Sellars, a director
William Shakespeare

SCENE

Backstage

(As the house lights dim the final speech, in a production in progress, of Shakespeare's "Richard The Third" is heard in the distance.)

RICHMOND: Let them not live to taste this land's increase,
That would with treason wound this fair land's peace!
Now civil wounds are stopp'd, peace lives again;
That she may long live here, God say amen!

(The sound of trumpets and applause is heard as the stage lights come up and SHAKESPEARE enters, followed by JOANNE.)

JOANNE: Well, sir. . . .

SHAKESPEARE: Please! Call me Will. It never did occur to Her Majesty to grant me a knighthood.

JOANNE: Well. . . . Will . . . what did you think?

SHAKESPEARE: Very interesting.

JOANNE: You're not being honest with me. I'd really like to know what you think.

SHAKESPEARE: Well, it's all so new to me.

JOANNE: The cuts.

SHAKESPEARE: Oh, I didn't mind the cuts. I wasn't even aware of them. I was very impressed with the theatre. And the audience. They were so polite.

JOANNE: Of course, the American accent.

SHAKESPEARE: It wasn't the accent so much. So many of the words were slurred. And they should speak up.

JOANNE: Naturalism.

SHAKESPEARE: Oh.

JOANNE: We like our theatre to be lifelike.

SHAKESPEARE: Oh, by all means. I quite agree.

JOANNE: Though, of course, the words are important. What did you think of the setting?

SHAKESPEARE: Well—.

JOANNE: You didn't care for it.

SHAKESPEARE: It's not important, really. Was there something special about it?

JOANNE: Well, yes. It's symbolic, you see.

SHAKESPEARE: Oh, I see. What was the setting?

JOANNE: A junkyard.

SHAKESPEARE: A junkyard. Yes, yes, I know what a junkyard is. I'm a little confused. Why would you set "Richard The Third" in a junkyard? It's symbolic, yes, I understand. Your point of view of the world. I'm not quite sure what that has to do with "Richard The Third." But I'm sure you have your reasons.

JOANNE: "Richard The Third" has been produced quite a number of times since it was written, you see. I mean this is the twentieth century. I mean why do "Richard The Third" if you can't bring something new to it? Not that it isn't well written. My God!

SHAKESPEARE: It needs to speak to the times.

JOANNE: Exactly. Of course, your play is timeless, in a sense, but setting it in a junkyard adds a certain dimension to it.

SHAKESPEARE: (*After a moment.*) We never did have any sets to speak of.

JOANNE: What did you think of Buckingham?

SHAKESPEARE: I thought she was quite good.

JOANNE: You had no objection then?

SHAKESPEARE: To what? To casting a woman in the role? Why not? Necessity is the mother of invention, and she was quite convincing.

JOANNE: I'm glad you approve. I was really concerned about that. It's so difficult to break down barriers.

SHAKESPEARE: Barriers?

JOANNE: Yes. Why should sex stand in the way of art?

SHAKESPEARE: Quite so. All our women were played by men.

JOANNE: Exactly.

SHAKESPEARE: Of course, we often yearned—. But then, we had problems enough.

JOANNE: Conventions are so foolish at times.

SHAKESPEARE: Exactly, and if you couldn't find a suitable actor for Buckingham, why not cast a woman?

JOANNE: Oh, no! You miss the point. Carol's one of our best actresses. Actors! Why distinguish? At any rate, she wanted to play Buckingham so why shouldn't she be allowed to play the role?

SHAKESPEARE: Oh, no. I quite agree, and, as I say, she was very convincing.

JOANNE: There were some people that strongly objected. They were offended by the beard.

SHAKESPEARE: Oh, well.

JOANNE: But I will not be pigeonholed!

SHAKESPEARE: Good for you! There's one thing though, that I did find very disturbing.

JOANNE: What was that?

SHAKESPEARE: Perhaps it was symbolic. But why was Richard black?

JOANNE: You found that disturbing.

SHAKESPEARE: Yes, very. I understand actors are not well paid, and it's difficult to find the proper actors for the proper roles.

JOANNE: Walter's a very fine actor.

SHAKESPEARE: I'm sure he is.

JOANNE: You didn't care for his performance.

SHAKESPEARE: Well, to tell you the truth, I was so distracted by his appearance.

JOANNE: I see.

SHAKESPEARE: Did I say something wrong?

JOANNE: No, no, no. If that's the way you feel.

SHAKESPEARE: What way?

JOANNE: It's a problem.

SHAKESPEARE: What is?

JOANNE: It seems to grow worse as the years go by.

SHAKESPEARE: I'm afraid you've lost me.

JOANNE: Racial prejudice.

SHAKESPEARE: Is that what we're discussing?

JOANNE: Why shouldn't Walter be allowed to play Richard The Third?

SHAKESPEARE: I'm not objecting to Walter.

JOANNE: What are you objecting to?

SHAKESPEARE: I'm objecting to the color of his skin.

JOANNE: Exactly.

SHAKESPEARE: But you have make-up now.

JOANNE: You'd like him to put on white face?

SHAKESPEARE: Is that a no-no?

JOANNE: I'm afraid you don't understand. You see, the blacks in our country have been abused, mistreated and ignored artistically for generation after generation. And some of our finest artists are black. Why shouldn't they have the same opportunity as anyone else to play the great roles of our literature? As a matter of fact, the reason we're doing this play is to give Walter an opportunity to play Richard.

SHAKESPEARE: I still don't understand. I mean I do understand in a sense. But—. Well, wasn't it humiliating for him to place that hump on his back?

JOANNE: Of course not. That was part of his characterization.

SHAKESPEARE: But white make-up would be humiliating.

JOANNE: Why should he be ashamed of the color of his skin?

SHAKESPEARE: But Richard was white. If he's going to play Richard—. I don't understand. Isn't it humiliating for him to play a white man?

JOANNE: He's not playing a white man. The color of his skin has nothing to do with it. This is not a realistic production. It's set in a junkyard.

SHAKESPEARE: Well, why did Miss Patrick put on a beard?

JOANNE: That was her choice, and mine. She was playing a man. You don't understand.

SHAKESPEARE: Well, yes. We had stars in those days, too. Burbage was overweight when he played Hamlet and I added a line so that no one might comment on it. I thought surely along the way you were going to explain why Richard The Third was black.

JOANNE: We wouldn't presume to rewrite your play.

SHAKESPEARE: And so no one's confused by this odd piece of casting.

JOANNE: Well, there are some purists—.

SHAKESPEARE: Myself among them, apparently.

JOANNE: I'm sorry you're displeased.

SHAKESPEARE: Displeased, confused and yes, I'm afraid, rather resentful. Not only are you rewriting my play, but you're rewriting English history.

JOANNE: As a director I feel I have a right to interpret your play as I see fit.

SHAKESPEARE: And as a playwright I feel that the actor should adapt himself to the role—as Miss Patrick did—and not vice versa.

JOANNE: I'm sorry you're that narrow minded. Can't you see? We're trying to create a new milieu. An artistic milieu that is color blind.

SHAKESPEARE: You're not serious.

JOANNE: You know perfectly well what I mean!

SHAKESPEARE: Then you're really not interested in doing "Richard The Third." You're interested in promoting some social issue which has nothing to do with my play.

JOANNE: How ironic, coming from you! If there's any playwright who deals with social issues—.

SHAKESPEARE: Look, there may still be time. Isn't there some other play you'd like to do?

JOANNE: This is our Shakespearean production. Each year we do one of your plays. And this year it's "Richard The Third."

SHAKESPEARE: May I make a suggestion?

JOANNE: If you must.

SHAKESPEARE: "Othello!!" (*He strides off.*)

CURTAIN

DREAMS

A Play in Two Acts

Our revels now are ended. These our actors
As I foretold you, were all spirits and
Are melted into air, thin air;
. . . . . . We are such stuff
As dreams are made on, and our little life
Is rounded with a sleep.

William Shakespeare
THE TEMPEST

CAST OF CHARACTERS

Archer Lowe
Lily Fairmont
Fritz
Hilda

SCENE

A sitting room in the country home of the Lowes.

For Alfred Lunt and Lynn Fontanne

ACT I

Scene 1

(A morning in June. VOICES are heard Offstage. Apparently a GROUP OF PEOPLE are leaving after a visit. The VOICES fade and LILY FAIRMONT and ARCHER LOWE enter from the outside. THEY are well into middle age.)

LILY: I'm absolutely exhausted.

ARCHER: Let me get you some coffee. I'll put up a fresh pot.

LILY: I think there's still some left from breakfast.

(ARCHER goes into the kitchen. LILY sinks onto the sofa with a sigh, closes her eyes and throws her head back against the pillows. The phone rings.)

LILY: Oh, God! (*SHE covers her ears and curls up in a foetal position.*)

ARCHER: (*Offstage.*) That's the phone, dear. (*After a moment HE enters.*) Aren't you going to answer it? Lily? What on earth are you doing?

LILY: Is it still ringing?

(The phone stops ringing.)

ARCHER: No. It's stopped.

LILY: What? (*SHE takes her hands away from her ears.*)

ARCHER: I said it's stopped.

LILY: You needn't shout, dear. I'm not deaf.

ARCHER: Why didn't you answer the phone?

LILY: Because I don't want to speak to anyone.

ARCHER: It might have been important.

LILY: Why do I feel so exhausted?

ARCHER: It's all this inactivity. (*HE goes into the kitchen.*)

LILY: I could have sworn you said inactivity.

ARCHER: (*Offstage.*) What was that, dear?

LILY: I said, "I could have sworn you said inactivity."

ARCHER: (*Offstage.*) That's what I said, inactivity.

LILY: I think you've gone off your rocker. The farm work alone is enough to kill two horses. Plus a houseful of guests. I have never worked so hard in all my life.

ARCHER: (*Reenters.*) Movement is not necessarily activity.

LILY: Is that Oscar Wilde?

ARCHER: No, it's me. Archie Lowe.

LILY: That's rather profound, you know. We must give it to Bobby or Sam. Motion is not necessarily activity.

ARCHIE: Movement. I said movement is not necessarily activity.

LILY: Motion is better.

ARCHIE: Perhaps you're right.

LILY: Are you feeling well, dear?

ARCHIE: Yes. Yes, I'm feeling fine.

LILY: You're due for a check-up, you know. Now don't grumble. Harvey is an excellent doctor.

ARCHIE: I never said that he wasn't, but he can't perform miracles. A man with one kidney is a man with one kidney.

LILY: That's not nearly as profound. You may sit beside me and hold me.

(HE sits beside her and THEY snuggle.)

ARCHIE: What are you thinking?

LILY: I don't think you want to know.

ARCHIE: I hope you're not too lonely after I'm gone.

LILY: And what makes you so sure that you'll be the first to go?

ARCHIE: My dear Lily, you've always had the last word, haven't you?

LILY: Well, I'll be damned if you'll upstage me that much. Do you think I should leave my body to science? That would be the brave thing to do. At least, my eyes.

ARCHIE: What about your brain?

LILY: One really should do something useful with one's body.

ARCHIE: I think you have.

LILY: Don't be smutty. I'm perfectly serious. Let's both leave our eyes to the eye bank.

ARCHIE: Must we decide that now?

LILY: Yes, of course. One must make these decisions while one still has one's wits about one. Well, you can do what you like, but I'm leaving my eyes to the eye bank.

ARCHIE: What about your hair?

LILY: Don't be silly.

ARCHIE: You could keep growing it and donating wigs to posterity. It keeps growing after you're dead, you know. I wonder how long after.

LILY: All right, Archie. That's enough. Let's call Leslie.

ARCHIE: Why the hell not!

LILY: Hand me the phone, dear. What time is it there now?

ARCHIE: Two o'clock. (*HE hands the phone to LILY.*)

LILY: He'll be taking his afternoon siesta.

ARCHIE: We'll wake him up. Serve him right. Do you know the number?

LILY: Of course, I know the number. Good Lord, I should know the number by now. (*SHE dials the Operator.*) Hello, Myrtle. It's me, Lily.

Lily Fairmont. (*To ARCHIE, her hand over the mouthpiece.*) I think she's getting deaf. She always used to recognize my voice. (*Into phone.*) We want to call Leslie Torrance. No, dear, it's just outside of London. The number is Nottingham seven three nine two.

ARCHIE: Three.

LILY: (*To ARCHIE.*) What, dear?

ARCHIE: Seven three nine three.

LILY: (*Into phone.*) Seven three nine two.

ARCHIE: You're wrong.

LILY: (*to ARCHIE.*) You're thinking of his London flat. That ends in a three.

ARCHIE: So does the Vicarage. They both end in a three.

LILY: (*Into phone.*) Yes, dear. That'll be fine. (*SHE hangs up*). The lines are all tied up. She'll get back to us. Where are you going?

ARCHIE: Coffee. (*HE goes into the kitchen.*) What do you want for lunch?

LILY: Lunch? I haven't digested my breakfast yet. It's only ten o'clock.

ARCHIE: (*Offstage.*) How about a vegetable salad? I've got a new dressing I want to try. A fruit aspic. Iced tea. The herb tea you like so much.

LILY: Archie, I don't want to think about food. I've got to lose ten pounds.

ARCHIE: (*Enters with two mugs of coffee.*) Why?

LILY: Because I'm too heavy, and so are you.

ARCHIE: Speak for yourself, madam.

LILY: (*Accepting coffee.*) Thank you, dear.

ARCHIE: It just occurred to me.

LILY: What?

ARCHIE: That phone call. It might have been my fertilizer.

LILY: Fertilizers don't make phone calls, dear.

ARCHIE: I wish you had answered it.

LILY: You can call Henry if you like.

ARCHIE: I've been calling him every day for the past two weeks. You would think that fertilizer would be easy to come by.

LILY: Well, it is a very special one, isn't it, dear?

ARCHIE: So they say. It's really very frustrating. This is the first year that I've ever had any trouble with my string beans. No wise cracks.

LILY: Look at all the trouble I'm having with my French.

ARCHIE: You're simply not a linguist, Lily.

LILY: I'm determined to master it. Remember how Laurette used to rattle it off.

ARCHIE: That was before she took to the bottle.

LILY: Poor Laurette.

ARCHIE: I never liked Laurette.

LILY: Yes, dear, I know.

ARCHIE: She was destructive . . .

LILY: But she did give me my start.

ARCHIE: If it hadn't been her it would have been someone else.

LILY: What do you mean by that? I should have gone to see her. They say she was glorious. But she did hurt me so. Things were never the same after that dreadful evening. Isn't it funny! I feel closer to her now than when she was alive . . .

ARCHIE: That's because she can't answer back.

LILY: It's hard to think of Laurette as dead. She was life itself. I should have gone to see her when she was down and out. We were just a few blocks away.

ARCHIE: Lily, you made your peace with her. She understood.

LILY: No. She was very bitter. She never forgave me.

ARCHIE: Why are you so morbid this morning?

LILY: I don't know. All week long I've been thinking about Laurette. Ellen sent me some old photographs. Pictures of myself and Laurette and Matthew. There was one at a costume ball. We were dressed as harlequins. Are you all right?

ARCHIE: Yes, yes, I'm fine. Where shall we go this Fall?

LILY: Where would you like to go?

ARCHIE: We could go to Paris. It might help your French.

LILY: And your cooking. You've been dying to take that course. . . .

ARCHIE: I am weak on desserts.

LILY: What are you thinking, dear?

ARCHIE: That awful play!

LILY: It is awful, isn't it?

ARCHIE: It's sick.

LILY: Well, I wouldn't go that far. It's no sicker than Nietsche or Schopenhauer.

ARCHIE: Nietsche died in a madhouse.

LILY: What about Schopenhauer?

ARCHIE: It's not right for me, at all.

LILY: Do I look like a madam?

ARCHIE: There are all sorts of madams. She is the height of sophistication.

LILY: That's true.

ARCHIE: What would our public say?

LILY: Do we still have a public?

ARCHIE: Yes, of course, we do. There was a letter in the Times just a few weeks ago, I believe. "Whatever happened to the Lowes?"

LILY: That was almost a year ago, dear.

ARCHIE: Did I tell Fritz to stop at the feed store?

LILY: I'm sure you did.

ARCHIE: Well, I hope he remembers.

LILY: Will you stop worrying about your stringbeans?

ARCHIE: What else have I got to worry about? Did I say something wrong?

LILY: No, no.

ARCHIE: You looked at me so strangely. We are retired, aren't we? Aren't we?

LILY: Are you asking me or telling me?

ARCHIE: Both.

LILY: Yes, of course, we're retired. I couldn't face another tour.

ARCHIE: Not in that play, at any rate.

LILY: In any play.

ARCHIE: We should have made more films.

LILY: You're joking.

ARCHIE: No, no. I'm not. We could be respectable character actors today . . . "Also starring . . ."

LILY: "Also starring?" I shall never be an also starring. It's either Lily Fairmont in—or nothing. We've had it all, my dear. Why should we want to go back? Thirty years of stardom is enough for anyone.

ARCHIE: Thirty-three.

LILY: We should have done more classics.

(THEY sip their coffee in silence.)

LILY: Monty was buried this morning.

ARCHIE: Yes, I know. What a tragedy. He was forty-three.

LILY: Was he that old? Such a talented boy. Why do you think he fell to pieces like that?

ARCHIE: Why did Laurette fall to pieces? I've always maintained that character is more important than talent.

LILY: We mustn't judge anyone.

ARCHIE: Good Lord, Lily, I'm not judging anyone. I just find it difficult to have patience with fools. Life is too short. What a morbid morning! How did we get started on all of this? Oh, yes, my check-up. Well, I'm not going all the way to Chicago for a check-up. If you want me to have a check-up you can invite Harvey out here for a visit.

LILY: A check-up should be done in the office where he has all his instruments.

ARCHIE: Then I'll have one in the Fall—on the way to Paris.

LILY: Are we going to Paris?

ARCHIE: You said you wanted to go.

LILY: No, dear. That was you.

ARCHIE: Don't you want to go to Paris? We could be there in time for the new fashions. You could buy yourself a dress.

LILY: I haven't bought a dress in years.

ARCHIE: Then it's time you did.

LILY: What on earth for? I never wear the things I have. What are these scripts doing here?

ARCHIE: I was just leafing through them.

LILY: Good Lord, here's a copy of "Lucy Ann."

ARCHIE: That goes a long way back.

LILY: With all my notes. (*Reading.*) "Watch your toes in this scene."

ARCHIE: Your toes?

LILY: Don't you remember? Everyone used to tell me that I was pigeon-toed.

ARCHIE: Nonsense. You were never pigeon-toed.

LILY: You never noticed.

ARCHIE: You used to stick your neck forward, like a goose.

LILY: I still do.

ARCHIE: Well, you do it more gracefully now.

LILY: Oh, my. It wasn't a very good play, was it?

ARCHIE: Nobody ever said it was.

LILY: Of course they did. The critics raved.

ARCHIE: About you.

LILY: And about the play.

ARCHIE: Well, I suppose it was good for its day.

LILY: If something's good it's good. And here's a copy of "Victoria and Albert."

ARCHIE: How did that get in there?

LILY: This is still good. Oh my, what a lovely scene this was. Is.

ARCHIE: Our first triumph as a team.

LILY: God, how we worked in those days!

ARCHIE: Was that before or after the union?

LILY: Good Lord, Archie, that was long before Equity.

ARCHIE: Then why did we work so hard?

LILY: Because we were fools—and because we were in love.

ARCHIE: Whatever became of Mary Jennings?

LILY: She married that man in New Jersey, didn't she?

ARCHIE: Oh, yes.

LILY: They had us over for dinner once.

ARCHIE: Pork chops.

LILY: Good Lord, do you remember that?

ARCHIE: I was sick for a week.

LILY: Didn't we get a letter from her recently?

ARCHIE: I hope it wasn't a dinner invitation. How could she give it all up like that?

LILY: He was a banker, or something like that.

ARCHIE: You could have done much better yourself.

LILY: I don't think so. After I'm gone I want you to marry again.

ARCHIE: All right.

LILY: No, I mean it. People who are happily married usually do—

(HE looks at her quizzically.)

LILY: Remarry.

ARCHIE: Let me see—. Who shall it be? Would you care to choose your successor?

LILY: Not really, no. Oh, well, I suppose it might as well be Jean.

ARCHIE: Jean's an old lady.

LILY: She always did have a crush on you. She's never forgiven me for taking you away from her.

ARCHIE: What nonsense! She and Harry were very much in love.

LILY: Then why did he drink himself to death?

ARCHIE: He liked to drink.

LILY: You were very much more suited to each other—artistically, that is.

ARCHIE: We *were* awfully good together, weren't we?

LILY: Of course, I've always felt that she was very limited. I mean she's always Jean Courtney. Don't you think so? And I think it was disgraceful the way she clung to you—at the funeral. It was as if she were marking you as her next victim.

ARCHIE: Lily, that's indecent. Besides, that was fifty years ago.

LILY: Well, she's still very much alive. And I don't think it's funny.

ARCHIE: It's very gratifying, my dear, to note that after all these years you can still be jealous.

LILY: Well, you're still an attractive man.

ARCHIE: Nonsense. I was never really a leading man. My eyes are too small. My nose is too large. My chin is weak—

LILY: It is not weak. It's just a little indecisive, that's all. We should have been playwrights—like Beaumont and Fletcher—or Kaufman and Hart. As it is, we're barely a footnote in the history of the American theatre. Leslie Torrance will be performed a hundred years from now.

ARCHIE: One still remembers Burbage.

LILY: For being overweight.

ARCHIE: We are the chronicle of our time.

LILY: A chronicle is a newspaper, and you know what one does with old newspapers.

ARCHIE: What's gotten into you? What one is that?

LILY: "Night Follows Day."

ARCHIE: Does it hold up?

(LILY sighs.)

ARCHIE: What's the matter now?

LILY: Nothing. I was just remembering Monty and how sweet he was, and how vulnerable.

ARCHIE: Well, he's dead.

LILY: I know he's dead. Do you think we may have failed him in some way? He worshipped you, you know.

ARCHIE: He did no such thing. All right, I failed him. I should have taken him in and nursed him. I should have dried him out. I should have straightened out his sex life. I should have forced him to turn down all those movie offers and come back to the stage.

LILY: If I had been a man I would have taken him under my wing.

ARCHIE: Lily, he was a boy when he worked with us. We did what we could for him.

LILY: I just want a clear conscience when I meet my maker.

ARCHIE: Lily, I promise you, you shall be an angel.

LILY: I'm much too tall. At least, I was the last time they were casting angels.

ARCHIE: It's no use. We've got to find a play.

LILY: I have no objection to doing a play, but I'm not going to do just anything.

ARCHIE: You're quite right. The world is changing and we've got to keep in step.

LILY: I always thought we tried to keep one step ahead.

ARCHIE: You know perfectly well what I mean. I'm not going to do another piece of fluff.

LILY: Now really, just because Leslie is out of fashion—.

ARCHIE: I'm not discussing Leslie. Besides Leslie hasn't written a thing in years. All right. One short piece.

LILY: A very brave little piece.

ARCHIE: And it's been done. Besides, I want to speak to the young. The old will come to see us out of sentiment.

LILY: I wonder.

ARCHIE: Of course, they will. If not sentiment, curiosity. Is the magic still there? Was it ever there? Were the Lowes just a figment of our youth?

LILY: You could do Lear.

ARCHIE: And what would you play? Cordelia?

LILY: Regan.

ARCHIE: Over my dead body. With you as my daughter I'd have to be a hundred.

LILY: Lear is eighty, I believe. Regan could be thirty-five. Maybe forty.

ARCHIE: And what would that make Cordelia?

LILY: He could have had Cordelia from a second marriage. I was just thinking of you, my dear. You said you wanted to do a classic.

ARCHIE: A classic. Not an antique. Did you feed the chickens this morning?

LILY: What do you think I was doing while you were making breakfast?

ARCHIE: Well, you did forget last week.

LILY: I have never forgotten to feed the chickens. There was that day that I thought I had forgotten, but it turned out that I had.

ARCHIE: I'm going to work on the vegetables. What are you going to do?

LILY: Never you mind.

ARCHIE: You're not!

LILY: I most certainly am! And I think you ought to join me.

ARCHIE: Lily, the time to write one's autobiography is when one sees the writing on the wall.

LILY: Exactly.

ARCHIE: Well, we're not there yet. Not by a long shot. You're not going to tell everything, are you?

LILY: Don't be a fool! I'll tell them exactly what I think they'd like to hear.

ARCHIE: Exactly. And it won't be worth the paper that it's printed on. If we're going to write a book it's got to be the truth.

LILY: You mean I've got to tell my age?

ARCHIE: Exactly!

LILY: But I've forgotten how old I am.

ARCHIE: I haven't.

LILY: You don't know.

ARCHIE: Oh, yes I do. I looked it up when we went to visit your sister.

LILY: Where?

ARCHIE: In the town records.

LILY: You didn't!

ARCHIE: I most certainly did!

LILY: You mean you didn't believe me?

ARCHIE: It kept changing all the time. (*HE reaches out to touch her.*)

LILY: No, don't. I'm really very angry with you. Even Harvey doesn't know. You know more about me than I do myself. . . .

ARCHIE: I always have.

LILY: You won't tell anybody, will you?

ARCHIE: I will, if you persist in writing that book.

LILY: I do think we ought to leave some sort of record. Permanent, I mean.

ARCHIE: Well, there is our film.

LILY: Is that the way you want to be remembered?

ARCHIE: It's not that bad.

LILY: It's not that good.

ARCHIE: Why don't we collect our reviews and put them in a book?

LILY: You're not serious, are you?

ARCHIE: Why not? I think it's an excellent idea and we could write a running commentary—about each production.

LILY: I want to write about myself—Lily Fairmont.

ARCHIE: You're not Lily Fairmont. You're Lucretia Fairmont.

LILY: That's how much you know—you and your spying. I've been Lily Fairmont for years.

ARCHIE: Well, you were born Lucretia.

LILY: When I was born I weighed six pounds. What does that prove? Some of us have improved since then. It's all because of what that nasty man said.

ARCHIE: What is?

LILY: This restlessness. I think we've earned our retirement. "Tired Leslie Torrance" indeed! The greatest writer of comedy since Oscar Wilde! We've done Shakespeare, we've done Chekov, we've done Shaw.

ARCHIE: O'Neill, Sherwood, Behrman. How many years of repertory? There isn't a goddamned milk stop in this country that we haven't played.

LILY: We are Theatre to millions and millions and millions.

ARCHIE: Werfel and Rattigan.

LILY: And Tarkington and Kaufman.

ARCHIE: And Giradoux.

LILY: And Werfel.

ARCHIE: I said Werfel. Besides nobody remembers Werfel anymore.

LILY: We've forgotten Molnar and Maxwell Anderson.

ARCHIE: And Ben Jonson.

LILY: Repertory indeed! We pioneered repertory.

ARCHIE: But what have we done lately?

LILY: Well, if you feel up to it and we find the right play, I have no objection, but I will not play a madam—who smokes a cigar.

ARCHIE: Do I look like a grocer?

LILY: A grocer, at least, is respectable.

ARCHIE: Do you realize that we keep coming back to this goddamned play?

LILY: Only because the two starring roles are equally important.

ARCHIE: Now you know that isn't true. The play is a brilliant piece of work.

LILY: I never said that it wasn't.

ARCHIE: It's haunting. And, I suppose, in its own ugly way, it is even beautiful. That is quite an entrance you make.

LILY: What is the point of making a negative statement?

ARCHIE: Cynical, not negative. It's a parable. Like Aesop.

LILY: Aesop wrote fables.

ARCHIE: There are many recesses of the human heart. Not all of them are sweetness and light. Look at poor Monty—and Laurette. Lily?

LILY: Yes, dear?

ARCHIE: Let's do the play.

LILY: Let's think about it, dear.

ARCHIE: Of course, we did turn it down. They may ask someone else.

LILY: Well, that's all that's important, isn't it? That the play be done.

ARCHIE: Quite right. I can think of all sorts of people who could play those parts.

LILY: Who—for example?

ARCHIE: Helen Carter.

LILY: Boring.

ARCHIE: And Tom Emerson.

LILY: Hammy! Can you see Helen Carter playing a madam?

ARCHIE: Well, she's got to have dignity.

LILY: Helen Carter could fornicate on stage and it would still be dull.

ARCHIE: Do you think she still does?

LILY: Not with Myron she doesn't.

ARCHIE: Maybe we ought to call them.

LILY: Who?

ARCHIE: Oliver! Oliver Jeffries!

LILY: Most certainly not. If they really want us, they will be in touch.

ARCHIE: Well, we did say "no" in no uncertain terms.

LILY: If they discourage that easily then I wouldn't want to work for them. Would you? I really should get to work—on my autobiography.

ARCHIE: Have you started it?

LILY: Well, of course, I've started it. What do you think I've been doing with that contraption?

ARCHIE: A tape recorder?

LILY: What do you suggest I use? A goose quill?

ARCHIE: On parchment paper.

LILY: Everyone talks into those things. People learn their lines with tape recorders.

ARCHIE: What will they think of next?

LILY: (*Produces a small portable cassette from a drawer.*) Don't you have anything to do?

ARCHIE: I'd like to hear this.

LILY: Well, you're not. Until it's edited.

ARCHIE: And who's going to do the editing? Not you?

LILY: Why not? It's like writing a letter. A letter to posterity. I think that's what I shall call it.

ARCHIE: What?

LILY: A letter to posterity.

ARCHIE: Don't you think that's rather pretentious?

LILY: I'm open to suggestions. Constructive ones.

ARCHIE: Would you like some more coffee? (*HE picks up the cups.*)

LILY: No, thank you, dear. Do go about your work.

ARCHIE: Very well. I know when I'm not wanted. If you need any help, just yell. I mean in regard to facts and figures.

LILY: I'm not concerned with figures.

ARCHIE: Nor facts, I'll wager. I'm gone. I'm gone.

(ARCHIE goes Off to the kitchen, with the coffee cups. LILY sighs and paces about. SHE walks about the room straightening things. SHE picks up a book, opens it and is absorbed. ARCHIE reenters.)

LILY: Now what?

ARCHIE: I was just passing through.

LILY: Then please do so. Yes? What is it?

ARCHIE: You're reading. I'm gone. I'm gone.

(ARCHIE goes Off to the outside. LILY presses the recording button.)

LILY: Shit. (*SHE presses the stop and rewinds the button and plays the machine. We hear LILY's VOICE say "Shit." SHE stops the machine.*) Well, at least, I know it's working. (*SHE moves about.*) Oh, this is awful! What torture! (*SHE records.*) Oh, this is awful! What torture! (*SHE plays the lines back then stops the machine.*) I'm not getting anywhere. (*SHE records.*) Actresses are born, not made. (*SHE stops the machine then records.*) Actresses are made, not born. (*SHE stops the machine.*) Oh, who cares? I'm not a writer. I never was and I never will be. That's it. (*SHE records.*) I'm not a writer and I never will be. (*SHE stops the machine.*) This is a waste of time. (*SHE lays aside the tape recorder and picks up a book.*) Je suis, tu es, il est, elle est. Nous sommes, vous ettes, ils sont. Je suis une belle femme. N'est pas? Pourquoi pas? Vous ettes un laid homme.

(The phone rings and SHE answers it.)

LILY: Hello? Hello? Oh, Leslie, I was never so glad to hear from anyone. No, no, no. Everything's fine. I know it's your siesta time, but we just had to speak to you. We miss you. Is that good enough? Frankly, dear, I'm rather concerned about Archie. He hasn't been up to snuff and he won't go in for a check up. Oh, dear. What does the doctor say? Well, have it removed. I see. Well, how can it bother you then? Oh Lord, that too?! Well, you can't have that removed. Oh, you can. Well, that's no fun. He's outside. Probably working on his string beans. You know how intense he gets about his vegetables. No, we turned that down. Well, really! You mean they're using our names to get the money. Well, that's what it amounts to. It's a brilliant piece. It's just that—. Don't you dare say a thing to Archie. I'll deny it, if you do—but I don't think he's up to it. Physically, I mean.

(ARCHIE enters from the outside.)

LILY: Archie, dear, it's Leslie.

ARCHIE: What?

LILY: On the phone. It's Leslie. Are you all right?

ARCHIE: I came in for my hat. The sun is very hot. (*HE takes the phone.*) You missed a magnificent breakfast, old boy. (*Claps his hand over the mouthpiece.*) Lily, would you be a dear and see if you can find my hat? I think I left it in the bedroom.

LILY: Yes. Yes, of course. (*SHE goes upstairs.*)

ARCHIE: Leslie, I want you to do me a favor. Oliver Jeffries is in London, I believe. He wanted us for that awful play. Well, we've changed our minds. Would you ring him and tell him—. Oh? Is he really? Are you sure?

(LILY reenters and hands ARCHIE his hat.)

ARCHIE: Thank you, dear. Leslie, I'll put Lily on again.

(HE hands the phone to Lily.)

LILY: When are you coming out? Then we'll see you in the fall. And do take care of yourself. Well, do the best you can. I love you, too. (*SHE hangs up.*)

ARCHIE: Did you know that Oliver has been using our name to raise money?

LILY: That's unethical.

ARCHIE: Of course, we have changed our minds. Haven't we?

LILY: Have we?

(ARCHIE puts on his hat and starts for the kitchen.)

LILY: Where are you going?

(HE looks about in confusion. The phone rings.)

ARCHIE: That will be Fritz with my fertilizer.

(LILY picks up the phone.)

LILY: Hello? Oliver! (*To ARCHIE.*) Speak of the devil! (*On the phone.*) How are you, dear? We're just fine.

ARCHIE: Let me speak to him.

LILY: What's that? I'll let you speak to Archie.

(SHE hands the phone to ARCHIE.)

ARCHIE: Oliver! How nice of you to think of us! Oh, I don't know. It's a brilliant play. No doubt about it. But how will it go down? Who? Yes, of course, I've heard of him. He's rather young, isn't he? Well, that's very kind of him. Well, of course, we'd be willing to meet with him, but I'm not making any promises. When? That'll be fine. Fine. Lily?

(LILY shakes her head.)

ARCHIE: She just stepped out. I most certainly will. And give my love to—ah—.

LILY: Margaret.

ARCHIE: Margaret. Good bye, Oliver. (*HE hangs up.*) Paul Baxter will be dropping by next week.

LILY: Paul Baxter?

ARCHIE: He's that bright young man—.

LILY: I know who he is. But why is he dropping by?

ARCHIE: He's directing.

LILY: I see.

ARCHIE: They're aiming to start the end of August.

LILY: So soon? Where?

ARCHIE: I don't know.

LILY: Well, I think we should certainly have something to say about that.

ARCHIE: We will, my dear, we will. I think the play has a better chance in England. Don't you?

LILY: Sweden.

ARCHIE: Sweden? Why Sweden?

LILY: They have the highest suicide rate. Let's face it, Archie, that play is morbid.

ARCHIE: So's Eugene O'Neill.

LILY: And we swore we would never do another O'Neill.

ARCHIE: And we haven't.

(A car horn is heard.)

LILY: That must be Fritz with our food—and your fertilizer. Come along.

(SHE goes out the front door. ARCHIE starts after her rather unsteadily. HE almost falls and catches on to a piece of furniture for support. HE remains still for a moment, trying to gain his equilibrium.)

LILY: (*Offstage.*) Archie?

ARCHIE: Coming, dear. I'm coming.

(HE straightens up and walks out the front door, weaving slightly.)

END OF ACT I, SCENE 1

ACT I

Scene 2

(Noon. Three weeks later. LILY enters from inside the house, and goes about the room searching for something.)

LILY: Archie? Archie?

ARCHIE: (*Offstage.*) Yes, dear?

LILY: Have you seen that tape recorder?

(ARCHIE enters.)

ARCHIE: Not recently no . . . How many scripts did I send for?

LILY: Six, I believe.

ARCHIE: That's what I thought. I've only got five. That's including the two we had.

LILY: You sent one to Roger and one to Tom.

ARCHIE: Then one is missing.

LILY: You gave one to Paul.

ARCHIE: So I did. What time is my appointment with Harvey?

LILY: Ten o'clock.

ARCHIE: That's good. How long do you think he'll poke around at me?

LILY: Well, I would certainly give myself a couple of hours. Why?

ARCHIE: I made a luncheon date with Roger, for one.

LILY: I don't think there should be any problem. Is he available? I said, "Is he available?".

ARCHIE: I heard you the first time.

LILY: Then why didn't you answer me?

ARCHIE: What do you think of Paul?

LILY: He's young.

ARCHIE: Everybody is these days.

LILY: Why? Do you think he'll be a problem?

ARCHIE: He's very insecure.

LILY: So am I.

ARCHIE: Yes, but he's afraid to admit it and that's easy to understand. I'm sure he's been told that nobody directs the Lowes.

LILY: Well, we've got to be fair to the boy.

ARCHIE: Fair? What has fair got to do with art?

LILY: Now, Archie—.

ARCHIE: What?

LILY: Nothing, dear.

ARCHIE: Don't do that to me, Lily. If you're going to say something, say it.

LILY: I just think that we've got to give the boy a chance.

ARCHIE: I want Roger for the Mayor.

LILY: And Tom for the School Master.

ARCHIE: What's wrong with that?

LILY: I think we ought to ask them both to read for Paul. Will you let me finish, please? First of all, it's only fair to Paul, since he is the director. And second of all, they may not be suitable to those parts.

ARCHIE: You're right.

LILY: You didn't hide that tape recorder on me, did you?

ARCHIE: Why would I do that?

LILY: Because if you did, I'll just go out and buy another one.

ARCHIE: Why?

LILY: Because I find it very useful for my French.

ARCHIE: Your French?

LILY: Yes, my French. Now, where is it? Archie?

ARCHIE: It's in the kitchen. Among the pots.

LILY: You are impossible. (*SHE goes into the kitchen.*)

ARCHIE: I don't want you learning your lines with that damn tape recorder.

LILY: (*Offstage.*) Why not?

ARCHIE: Because it's inhibiting. One begins to listen to oneself.

LILY: (*Offstage.*) Will you please come in here and find that damn tape recorder for me?

(*The phone rings.*)

LILY: I'll get the phone.

ARCHIE: (*Picks up the phone.*) Hello? Leslie, old boy. How are you feeling? Didn't Lily call you? We're doing the play. Well, Oliver called just after we spoke to you. I thought he called because of you.

(*LILY enters.*)

ARCHIE: Here's Lily. (*HE hands the phone to LILY.*) It's Leslie.

LILY: Hello, dear. (*To ARCHIE.*) He doesn't want to speak to me. He wants to speak to you.

ARCHIE: Tell him I went to the bathroom.

LILY: I will not. (*Into the phone.*) What's that? (*To ARCHIE.*) Besides, he heard you. (*SHE hands the phone to ARCHIE.*)

ARCHIE: Of course, I'm your friend. Leslie, please don't scold me. I shall weep. The tears are forming. They're about to drop. There goes one. Now see here, Leslie—. (*To LILY.*) He's crying.

LILY: (*Takes the phone.*) Darling, what is it? Oh, for God's sakes! How can you say that? How can you think that? Leslie, will you stop feeling sorry for yourself! Leslie, dear, there are worse things than death. I'm going to be very angry. (*SHE slams the phone down.*) I can't stand self pity in anyone. Least of all in Leslie Torrance.

ARCHIE: I thought you called him.

LILY: When?

ARCHIE: When we decided to do the play.

LILY: Do you think he's seriously ill?

ARCHIE: He has been for years.

LILY: I mean do you think he's dying.

ARCHIE: He wouldn't dare. Not before us.

LILY: We've got to spend some time with him.

ARCHIE: When?

LILY: Before we start rehearsals. We've got to find the time.

ARCHIE: I'm beginning to feel like the last leaf on the tree.

LILY: How do you think I feel?

ARCHIE: Work is the only answer. I feel ten years younger—at least.

LILY: Do you think I ought to call him back?

(The phone rings and LILY picks it up.)

LILY: Hello? Leslie, dear. We must have been cut off. It was all a misunderstanding. Archie thought that I had phoned you and I could have sworn that he did. No, we're taking it on tour. No, here in the States. Rehearsals start in September, just after Labor Day. When do you leave for St. Thomas? We were planning to spend some time with you. That'll work out beautifully. Yes, we're dying to read it. If you're going to be morbid—. That's better. We'll call you from New York. We should be there in a week or two. Goodbye, dear.

(SHE hangs up.)

LILY: He says he's rewritten "The Morning After."

ARCHIE: It's thin, thin, thin.

LILY: Let's keep an open mind, dear.

ARCHIE: How ill-kempt do you think Gunther ought to be?

LILY: Archie, where is that tape recorder?

(HE goes Off to the interior of the house.)

LILY: Archie, where are you going?

ARCHIE: (*Offstage.*) I forgot something.

LILY: Archie, the luggage is gone. There is no more room. I left half of my wardrobe behind because of all your pots and pans.

(HE reenters with an armful of scripts.)

LILY: What are those?

ARCHIE: Scripts. New plays.

LILY: I can see that. What do you intend to do with them?

ARCHIE: Read 'em, of course. We shall never be idle again.

(HE goes Off.)

LILY: Now where are you going? Archie, you're not going to take all of those scripts.

(HE reenters with another armful of scripts.)

ARCHIE: Why not?

LILY: What are you going to carry them in? There are no more trunks. There are no more suitcases.

ARCHIE: We'll put them in boxes. Cardboard boxes. We've got to find a comedy to follow this up. A good comedy. A serious comedy. A comedy with stature.

LILY: They don't write them anymore.

ARCHIE: Of course, they do. And it's our job to find new plays, new playwrights. Do we have any boxes?

LILY: I'm sure there must be some boxes somewhere.

ARCHIE: Good. I feel better already.

LILY: About what?

ARCHIE: Do you realize that we've been trying to drown ourselves in idleness? My God, we're not that old. I want to keep working. We've been half alive. Why go out to meet death? It'll find us soon enough.

LILY: Do you really want to drive all the way to Chicago?

ARCHIE: Why not?

LILY: Suppose you get a dizzy spell?

ARCHIE: I'll pull over to the curb. I'm perfectly fine.

LILY: Well, frankly, dear, I don't feel very secure with you at the wheel. I'm sorry, dear, but I don't. I don't see why Fritz can't drive us down, or we can take the train. All right, all right, then let Fritz drive us.

ARCHIE: Fritz has enough to take care of right here.

LILY: Where are you going?

ARCHIE: To find some boxes. (*HE goes into the kitchen.*) Did you buy a present for Jenny's baby?

LILY: When did I have time? We won't be seeing them for a couple of days.

ARCHIE: (*Offstage.*) What did we do with those sandwiches?

LILY: They're in the car.

ARCHIE: (*Offstage.*) What did you say?

LILY: I said the lunch is in the car. Everything is in the car, except us, and those manuscripts—. I hope.

(ARCHIE reenters with a cardboard box.)

ARCHIE: Are we flying to New York or taking the train?

LILY: I thought we were flying. Where did you get that box?

ARCHIE: In the pantry. It had all sorts of cans in it.

LILY: What kind of cans?

ARCHIE: I mean jars.

LILY: What did you do with the jars?

ARCHIE: I set them on the floor. This box will do fine.

LILY: Archie, I wish you'd sit down and rest for a minute.

ARCHIE: What for?

LILY: You've been working like a fiend these past two weeks. We've still got a long drive ahead of us. Will you please sit down and let me pack the manuscripts?

(ARCHIE sits and LILY packs.)

ARCHIE: I don't want a shabby set.

LILY: But the town is shabby, to begin with.

ARCHIE: And it's got to be flexible. Easily flown. We don't want to be burdened down with clumsy pieces. Misha would have been perfect. The sort of thing he did for "The Wanderer."

LILY: Paul doesn't want Misha.

ARCHIE: I know Paul doesn't want Misha. He thinks that he's old-fashioned. He wants a stylized set—whatever that means. I just hope that we can recognize the pieces for what they are. I mean a church steeple has got to look like a church steeple and a train station has got to look like a train station and we didn't even discuss the lighting. I refuse to work in the dark. I don't care how gloomy this piece is, I insist on being seen. As a matter of fact, the gloomier the play the brighter the lights ought to be. Don't you agree?

LILY: Yes, of course I do, dear, but I'm not going to get excited unless I absolutely have to.

ARCHIE: I just think we have to be aware of these things. I made some sketches—.

LILY: You showed me the sketches.

ARCHIE: Well, what did you think of them?

LILY: They're very practical . . .

ARCHIE: That's all they were meant to be. I'm not an artist. And there's got to be some love somewhere in the play. I mean people have got to be able to identify with these characters somewhere along the line. Don't you agree? Don't just shake your head. Do you or don't you?

LILY: Yes, of course I do, dear. We always agree on everything.

ARCHIE: Since when? (*HE goes Off.*)

(LILY continues to pack the scripts. SHE opens one and sits reading it. ARCHIE reenters with some papers.)

ARCHIE: I really think we should have opened the play in the provinces.

LILY: We would have had to use all British actors.

ARCHIE: This union business is ridiculous. . . .

LILY: As I remember, dear, you were all for it.

ARCHIE: In principle, yes. But we can be protected out of existence.

LILY: Besides, it's British Equity not ours that we'd be dealing with, and please don't start cursing the Limey's.

ARCHIE: I have no intention of cursing anyone. Where are we going to stay in London?

LILY: If we're going to visit Leslie, we'll stay with him.

ARCHIE: If he's ill?

LILY: We'll stay at the Saxony.

ARCHIE: The Saxony no longer exists, my dear. It hasn't existed since World War Two. As a matter of fact, it was demolished the time we were staying there.

LILY: Yes, I remember. At two in the morning. That was the night you took those awfully long pauses. Thank God. (*Finishes packing the scripts.*) There! I hope you don't find anything else to take along. Are you all packed?

ARCHIE: I've just got to close my suitcase.

LILY: Then I suggest you do so, because Fritz ought to be back any minute now.

ARCHIE: What about you?

LILY: I'm all ready to go. What about those scripts? We're not going to take them with us to Chicago, are we?

ARCHIE: Why not? We can read them at bed time, at lunch time, at breakfast.

LILY: Even the ones we've done?

ARCHIE: We may want to revive one of them. You said yourself—.

LILY: All right, dear. All right.

ARCHIE: I can't believe it.

LILY: What?

ARCHIE: That we're working again. You are glad, aren't you?

LILY: I'll tell you after we open.

(ARCHIE goes Off to the bedroom.)

LILY: Now where are you going? I can't imagine what's happened to Fritz. We really ought to get started. Do you think we ought to call the train station. What on earth are you doing?

(ARCHIE reenters lugging a large suitcase.)

ARCHIE: Good Lord, what have you got in here? Rocks?

LILY: Archie, dear, Fritz can load the car. . . .

ARCHIE: I thought we were keeping only our necessities with us. . . .

LILY: Like a box of scripts?

ARCHIE: Exactly! (*HE goes Off to the bedroom.*)

LILY: Archie, dear—please. You're going to rupture yourself. (*The telephone rings and LILY answers it.* Hello? Oh, Fritz, what happened to you? I see. Yes. Yes, we're all ready. All right. (*SHE hangs up.*) Archie, that was Fritz. He had a flat tire. He'll be here any minute now. Archie? What on earth are you doing in there? (*SHE goes off to the bedroom. There is a pause and LILY reenters quickly and picks up the phone.*) Hello? Hello, Myrtle? There's something wrong with Mr. Lowe. Would you call the hospital and have them send an ambulance at once? I don't know. He's unconscious. Hurry, Myrtle, please.

(LILY hangs up, stands fearfully for a moment, then goes quickly off as the lights fade.)

END OF ACT I, SCENE 2

ACT II

Scene 1

(Six weeks later. Early afternoon. The phone rings. HILDA enters from the kitchen and answers it.)

HILDA: Hello? No, Mr. Torrance, they're not here yet. Any minute now. No, I haven't seen him yet. I'll have her call you when she gets in. (*SHE hangs up and starts for the kitchen. The phone rings again and SHE answers it.*) Hello? No, Mr. Jeffries, but they should be here very soon. (*SHE makes a note on a pad near the phone.*) Yes. Yes, I have the number. Till five o'clock. I'll tell her, Mr. Jeffries.

(The sound of a car is heard as HILDA hangs up. SHE starts for the outside door and suddenly remembers something.)

HILDA: Oh, my goodness!

(HILDA goes off to the kitchen. LILY enters from the outside, carrying an overnight bag.)

LILY: Hilda? We're back.

HILDA: (*Offstage.*) Coming, Miss Lily. (*SHE reenters.*) I forgot to turn off the soup. Where is he?

LILY: Fritz is driving him about—to take a look at things. Here, give me a hand. (*SHE produces a banner from her bag.*)

HILDA: What is it? Oh, isn't that nice! Why didn't you tell me? I would have made you one.

(The banner reads "Welcome Home, Archie".)

LILY: I had nothing to do with my nights and I really wasn't up to seeing people.

HILDA: Where shall we put it?

LILY: I want him to see it as soon as he comes in.

HILDA: Yes. Yes, of course. It's lovely.

LILY: Well, it's colorful. I used to be very handy with the needle, when I had to be. What is it?

HILDA: You've lost some weight.

LILY: Yes, I know. I look awful.

HILDA: Is he all right now?

LILY: His condition is stable.

HILDA: What does that mean?

LILY: The right side of his body is paralyzed and his speech is very limited.

HILDA: Is that permanent?

LILY: Not if I can help it.

HILDA: What do the doctors say?

LILY: Anything is possible. A therapist will be coming by twice a week. A physical therapist. And we've got to work on his speech. The longer he remains the way he is, the less chance there is for his recovery.

HILDA: But a stroke, Miss Lily—. . . .

LILY: Just a broken blood vessel, that's all. There's no reason why he can't lead a normal life—eventually.

HILDA: But the brain—.

LILY: The brain is an organ. And organs heal themselves—.

HILDA: Yes. Yes, of course.

LILY: We're going to need lots of help.

HILDA: You can count on us.

LILY: I know I can, but I think it's going to take more than the three of us. He's going to need constant attention. Constant.

HILDA: I'm sure the neighbors—. Everybody loves Mr. Lowe.

LILY: Do you think so? I've made out a schedule.

HILDA: He's not a young man, Miss Lily. We mustn't expect miracles.

LILY: I don't see why not. I've created them all my life, and so has Mr. Lowe.

HILDA: He can be very stubborn, you know, especially when he's not feeling well.

LILY: Well, so can we. And I do know one thing. He doesn't want to remain the way he is.

HILDA: What way is that?

LILY: A vegetable. It's not that he's dead inside. His mind is working all right, but it's a prisoner. A prisoner in a body that isn't functioning properly. And that's going to be our job. To see that it does.

HILDA: Can he speak at all?

LILY: Barely. And most of what he says doesn't make any sense.

HILDA: But if his brain is damaged—.

LILY: Hilda, it can be done. It has to be done, because if it isn't, he will die. I know it. He won't want to live as he is now.

HILDA: I understand.

LILY: There have been many cases of partial recovery. Complete recovery, even after a doctor has given them up.

HILDA: What about the play?

LILY: What about it?

HILDA: Mr. Jeffries phoned twice today. He left a number where he can be reached until five o'clock.

LILY: It's out of the question.

HILDA: Poor Mr. Lowe. He had his heart set on doing that play.

LILY: Yes, I know.

HILDA: And so did you.

LILY: There will be other plays.

HILDA: It took you two years to find this one.

LILY: Well, in two years time we'll be ready to do another one.

HILDA: Have you told Mr. Jeffries?

LILY: I've tried to.

HILDA: He wants you very badly.

LILY: If he wants us badly enough he can wait two years. Maybe I'd better call him. I think the banner looks fine there, don't you?

HILDA: Yes. It's fine. I've got some lunch for you. Mr. Lowe likes my potato soup—and a little salad. How does he manage? With his eating, I mean?

LILY: Soup may be a problem.

HILDA: I'm baking some muffins, too. I'd better see how they're coming.

(HILDA goes into the kitchen. The phone rings.)

LILY: That's all right. I've got it. (*SHE picks up the phone.*) Hello? Yes, Myrtle. That's very kind of you. We're hoping he will improve—with therapy. Well, yes, as a matter of fact, there is something you could do. He'll need constant attention. It's a matter of communication. That's all it is. Very basic exercises—and discipline. Well, that would be very nice. I wouldn't want to impose. Well, actually he should be kept busy, at least five or six hours a day. Oh, Myrtle—would you ring—. Let me see—. 212-264-6565. Yes. Yes, I'll hold on.

(HILDA reenters.)

HILDA: Are you hungry?

LILY: I'm starved and I'm sure that Mr. Lowe's hungry, too. We might as well eat in here, Hilda.

HILDA: Yes, ma'am. (*SHE goes Off to the kitchen.*)

LILY: Hello? Thank you, Myrtle. (*SHE hangs up and picks up the pad, studying the messages.*) When did Mr. Torrance call?

HILDA: (*Offstage.*) A few minutes ago. He said he would call again. I put all the mail on your desk.

LILY: Thank you, dear.

(LILY goes Off to her room. The outside door is opened and ARCHIE, in a wheelchair, is wheeled in by FRITZ.)

FRITZ: There you are, Mr. Lowe, back home again.

(ARCHIE hammers angrily with his left hand against the side of the chair. FRITZ shuts the door as HILDA reenters.)

HILDA: Oh, Mr. Lowe, it's so good to have you back. You look wonderful. You really do.

(ARCHIE shakes his head.)

FRITZ: Mr. Lowe is doing fine. Aren't you, Mr. Lowe?

(ARCHIE bangs the chair.)

HILDA: What is it, Mr. Lowe?

FRITZ: He's just happy to be home again. Aren't you, Mr. Lowe?

ARCHIE: Cigarettes!

HILDA: What is it, Mr. Lowe?

ARCHIE: Cigarettes!

HILDA: Cigarettes? But you don't smoke, Mr. Lowe.

FRITZ: He's just having his little joke. Aren't you, Mr. Lowe?

ARCHIE: Cigarettes!! Cigarettes!!

HILDA: Is he allowed to smoke?

FRITZ: Well, one cigarette wouldn't hurt him. (*HE takes a pack from his pocket.*)

HILDA: I don't think so, Fritz.

FRITZ: Here you are, Mr. Lowe.

(ARCHIE knocks the pack out of his hand.)

HILDA: He doesn't want a cigarette. He must mean something else. Are you hungry, Mr. Lowe?

(ARCHIE nods.)

HILDA: He's hungry. He must want his lunch. Would you like to see the kitchen, Mr. Lowe?

(ARCHIE nods, and HILDA wheels him into the kitchen. FRITZ picks up his cigarettes as LILY reenters with the mail. . . .)

LILY: Where's Mr. Lowe?

FRITZ: He's in the kitchen with Hilda.

LILY: You're not going to smoke in here, are you, Fritz?

FRITZ: No, no. Mr. Lowe asked for a cigarette and when I gave them to him he knocked them out of my hand.

LILY: Mr. Lowe asked you for a cigarette?

FRITZ: He kept saying cigarette and hitting the side of the chair.

LILY: He was upset about something. You mustn't be condescending to him, Fritz. You mustn't treat him like a child.

FRITZ: I was just trying to be nice to him.

LILY: I know, I know. But he does have all his wits about him. It's just that he can't express himself. I know, I know. It's difficult to know what to say or what to do.

FRITZ: I'll do my best, Miss Lily.

LILY: I know you will, Fritz.

(HILDA wheels ARCHIE in.)

ARCHIE: Home!

LILY: Yes, dear.

HILDA: I just wanted to show Mr. Lowe that all his pots and pans are nice and shiny.

ARCHIE: Home.

LILY: I think he wants to say that he hopes to use them soon.

(ARCHIE nods. HILDA turns away to hide her tears.)

HILDA: I'll get your lunch. Shall I, Miss Lily?

LILY: Are you hungry, Archie?

(ARCHIE nods.)

LILY: We're ready for lunch.

(HILDA goes into the kitchen.)

LILY: Would you like a bath first, Archie, or a shower?

(ARCHIE shakes his head.)

FRITZ: I'll get the things out of the car. (*HE goes Off.*)

LILY: You haven't said a thing about my banner. That's all right. You don't have to. We've got all sorts of mail. Did you notice how well your string beans are doing? That new fertilizer did the trick.

ARCHIE: Now—Now—.

LILY: What, dear?

ARCHIE: Foooootal.

LILY: Fertilizer?

(ARCHIE nods and points to himself.)

LILY: A fertilizer for you? Yes, dear. That would be nice. We'll find one, my dear. We'll find one.

(ARCHIE shakes his head.)

LILY: Now, stop it. You're going to get better. You can move your foot, can't you? And your arm.

(ARCHIE shakes his head.)

LILY: Yes, you can. You did this morning. And it's only a matter of time and patience. You mustn't give up.

ARCHIE: Abba. Abba.

LILY: It is not hopeless! Now don't make me angry. And if you start to sulk I'll hit you over the head with your pots and pans.

ARCHIE: Abba.

LILY: (*Opening mail.*) We got a card from Mary Jennings and a lovely note. Here, why don't we open some? I'll read them to you.

(SHE places some of the mail on the tray of ARCHIE's wheelchair and starts to open a card.)

LILY: Come on dear. Just help me open them.

(ARCHIE pushes the mail onto the floor. LILY sighs and picks them up.)

LILY: All right, dear. You've made your point. You're hungry, aren't you.

(ARCHIE nods.)

LILY: Hilda has gone to get your lunch.

ARCHIE: Ha ba chada. He ba chada.

LILY: I don't know what you're saying, dear. All right, all right. Don't upset yourself. Oh, Archie, please. If you'll only be patient. You will improve, I promise you. But it's going to take time.

ARCHIE: No time.

LILY: There you are. That was nice and clear. You want to improve, don't you?

(ARCHIE nods.)

LILY: Then you will. Here comes your lunch.

(HILDA enters with a tray of food, which SHE places on the tray of the wheelchair.)

LILY: Could we have a large napkin?

HILDA: Certainly. (*She goes into the kitchen.*)

ARCHIE: Un un.

LILY: Now, Archie.

ARCHIE: Uh un!!

(HILDA reenters with a cloth napkin which SHE hands to LILY and goes back into the kitchen.)

LILY: Now hold still, dear.

ARCHIE: Un un!

(LILY manages to tuck the napkin into ARCHIE's collar. HE tears it off and throws it onto the floor.)

LILY: You're going to get food all over yourself.

ARCHIE: Un, un.

(SHE picks up the napkin as HILDA enters with a second tray of food which SHE places on the table.)

HILDA: That's all right, Miss Lily. We can change his shirt after he eats.

ARCHIE: Un un.

LILY: There's going to be a lot of laundry.

HILDA: I'll be happy to wash the extra shirts.

ARCHIE: Un un.

LILY: All *right*, dear. You've *made* your point.

(HILDA goes Off to the kitchen. ARCHIE starts to eat the soup with his left hand. HE has great difficulty.)

LILY: You must eat slowly, dear, if you want to get some into your stomach.

(ARCHIE points to LILY's food and then to her.)

ARCHIE: Un un.

(LILY sighs and starts to eat. HILDA reenters.)

HILDA: Is there anything you need? Oh, Mr. Lowe. You're leaking.

(*SHE takes the napkin and dabs ARCHIE's chin and mouth.*) I hope it's all right. The soup, I mean.

(ARCHIE nods.)

HILDA: There may be too much oregano.

(ARCHIE shakes his head.)

ARCHIE: Booboo. Booboo!

LILY: I think he means sugar.

HILDA: Oh, yes. I measured wrong. Would you like some salt?

(ARCHIE shakes his head.)

LILY: You're eating too fast, Archie. You'll give yourself indigestion.

ARCHIE: (*Bangs side of chair.*) Cigarettes! Cigarettes!

(HILDA holds the tray to prevent it from spilling.)

LILY: I don't want to fuss over you and I wouldn't if you behaved like a human being. Now damn it, eat slowly!

(ARCHIE eats in slow motion.)

LILY: That's better. The soup is very good, Hilda. The best you've ever made.

ARCHIE: Booboo.

HILDA: Except for the sugar.

LILY: Well, it's not too sweet for me.

HILDA: Would you like me to help you, Mr. Lowe?

(ARCHIE hands the spoon to HILDA and SHE feeds him the soup.)

HILDA: There you are. But you haven't eaten your muffin. May I cut it in quarters for you?

(ARCHIE nods.)

HILDA: Would you like a little butter on it?

(ARCHIE nods.)

HILDA: There you are. I didn't put too much dressing on the salad. If you'd like some more, just let me know.

(FRITZ enters from a room Stage Right.)

FRITZ: I put Mr. Lowe's things in the guest room.

ARCHIE: Ah—na.

LILY: Well, Archie, you can't climb the stairs.

ARCHIE: Ah—na.

(FRITZ starts Off.)

LILY: Oh, Fritz. You can put my bag in the guest room, too. I'll be sleeping there.

FRITZ: Sure, Miss Lily. (*HE goes Off.*)

LILY: We have all sorts of calls. Leslie called twice and Oliver and Jean and Misha and Tom. Paul Baxter. What, dear?

(ARCHIE shakes his head and HILDA spills some soup.)

HILDA: Oops. That's all right, Mr. Lowe. That's the end of the soup. Why don't you have some muffin and some salad?

(ARCHIE shakes his head.)

HILDA: I baked it especially for you.

(ARCHIE takes a bite of muffin and tries to speak with his mouth full . . . HE swallows the bite then tries to speak again.)

ARCHIE: Ssss. Ssss.

HILDA: Salt.

LILY: Say it, dear.

(ARCHIE shakes his head.)

LILY: You've said it before. Archie you can say salt. Very well. Take the muffin away from him.

ARCHIE: (*Bangs the chair.*) Cigarette! Cigarette!

LILY: And stop using that stupid word. You don't mean cigarette.

HILDA: That's all right, Miss Lily.

LILY: Take the muffin away from him.

(HILDA hesitates. LILY rises and goes for the muffin. ARCHIE seizes a piece and stuffs it into his mouth . . . HE starts to choke and spits it out.)

LILY: Are you quite through?

ARCHIE: Salt! Salt! Salt!

LILY: That's better. He mustn't be humored, Hilda. When he acts like a child, he must be treated like a child. If you don't try, you won't improve.

(ARCHIE starts to cry.)

LILY: And stop crying. I know you can cry. It's your speech I'm concerned about.

ARCHIE: Y—y—you—. . .

LILY: Yes? What am I?

ARCHIE: B-B-B-Bitch!

LILY: How about just plain bitch?

ARCHIE: Yes, bitch! (*HE pants with exhaustion from the effort.*)

(HILDA goes into the kitchen with the soup bowl.)

LILY: I am not going to let her baby you. There's no reason why you have to be fed.

(The phone rings and LILY answers it.)

LILY: Hello? Yes, Leslie, we're home. Yes, he's right here. He's eating his lunch. Very sloppily, I might add, but he's eating. How are you feeling? Well, you sound much better. Just a minute. (*To ARCHIE.*) He wants to talk to you. It's Leslie.

(ARCHIE shakes his head. . . .)

LILY: (*Into phone.*) It's very difficult for him to speak. (*To ARCHIE.*) He wants to speak to *you.* You don't have to answer him. Oh, for God sakes, Archie, take the phone.

(ARCHIE tries to wheel the chair with one hand and it starts to circle.)

LILY: Just a minute, Leslie. (*SHE puts down the phone and wheels ARCHIE to it. SHE picks up the receiver.*) Here he is, Leslie.

(ARCHIE takes the receiver and listens. HE starts to cry.)

LILY: Say something to him.

ARCHIE: L—L—Leslie—. Abba. Abba.

LILY: Thank him for calling.

ARCHIE: Home. Home.

(HE shakes his head and hands phone to LILY.)

LILY: Yes, Leslie. He heard you. I don't know. (*Pause.*) Leslie— (*Pause.*) I've got to be going, Leslie. I'll call you tomorrow. Goodbye, Leslie! (*SHE hangs up.*)

ARCHIE: Wh—wh—wh—what? L—Leslie? (*HE points to his mouth.*)

LILY: He asked about the play?

ARCHIE: Wha—wha—what?

LILY: He asked me what the plans for the play were? I said I didn't know.

(FRITZ enters from the other room.)

FRITZ: I put your suitcase in the room. Would you like me to unpack Mr. Lowe's things?

LILY: I suppose you might as well. And I think Mr. Lowe ought to have a bath. Maybe in an hour or so. Would you like a bath or a shower, Archie?

(HE shakes his head. SHE turns to FRITZ.)

LILY: I think a bath might be easier to handle.

ARCHIE: Abba. Abba.

LILY: If you're trying to say that you want a shower we'll have to wait on that.

(FRITZ starts Off to the room.)

LILY: Oh, Fritz, you might bring in the walker.

ARCHIE: Abba. Abba.

FRITZ: Yes, Miss Lily. (*HE goes Off.*)

LILY: You haven't walked all day.

ARCHIE: Abba. Abba.

LILY: I know you're anxious to and as soon as—.

ARCHIE: No!

LILY: No what?

ARCHIE: T—T—Tired.

LILY: You are no such thing. You slept the whole morning. And you missed your noontime exercises.

ARCHIE: Abba. Abba. Chada. Chabada be.

LILY: I don't know what you're trying to say, but we will skip your exercises for today. Only because the therapist is coming tomorrow and she may want to make some changes. But you will do some walking . . . And maybe we'll play a game of checkers. Don't look so pained. I have improved. Now, why don't you eat your salad, while I open some of these letters.

(ARCHIE picks at his salad.)

LILY: My goodness, here's a letter from the governor. Wasn't that nice of him? Shall I read it to you?

(ARCHIE shakes his head.)

LILY: Yes or no?

(ARCHIE shakes his head.)

LILY: Very well. (*Reads.*) "Dear Lily and Archer—"

ARCHIE: No!

LILY: You're quite right. It's a very dull letter. I don't suppose you want to hear what Jean has to say.

(ARCHIE nods.)

LILY: Does that mean yes or no?

ARCHIE: Weh.

LILY: Yes?

ARCHIE: Weh!

LILY: Yes! Very well. (*Reads.*) "Dear Archie—." You will notice that I am not included, which, I think is very rude of her.

ARCHIE: M—M—Me! (*Pointing to himself. . . .*)

LILY: Yes, I know it's addressed to you. You mean you're the one that's sick.

ARCHIE: (*Nods.*) W—W—Weh!

LILY: Yes. Well, at any rate—. "Dear Archie, I was devastated to learn about your illness." How dramatic! "As you know I have had many tragedies in my life and I'm still here. And I suppose that is the important thing, survival. I often wonder why, but then, on my good days, when the sun is shining and the birds are singing and I have my loved ones about, it all seems worthwhile. And, of course, there's my work." Eat your salad, dear.

ARCHIE: Y—Y—You! (*HE points to his mouth.*)

LILY: Well, I can't eat and read at the same time. Which would you prefer?

(ARCHIE points to his mouth.)

LILY: I don't know what that means, dear.

(HE points to his eyes.)

ARCHIE: Eeee . . . Eeee. Eed.

LILY: Eat?

(ARCHIE shakes his head.)

ARCHIE: R—R—R. Ead. R—R—Read.

LILY: Read.

(ARCHIE nods.)

LILY: Very well, if I must. "As you must have read by now, I'm working with the Tyrone Guthrie Repertory Company and I can't tell you how exciting it is. Not the repertory—which I hate, but the company. Young and Eager. It's like starting all over again. It takes me back to the days we worked together—" and I was madly in love with you.

ARCHIE: Aba.

LILY: No, she doesn't say that, but she certainly was.

ARCHIE: Ah—ah—ahbba.

LILY: "It takes me back to the days we worked together and we were both starting out. How exciting those days were! We were eager for challenge and adventure. Now it takes every ounce of me to keep up with these young devils, but they're all so kind to this old lady." This entire letter's all about her. Ah, now we come to the good part. (*SHE folds the letter and puts it back into the envelope.*) We'll save it. It'll be part of your exercise. You can read the rest of the letter to me.

(HILDA enters from the kitchen with two dessert dishes.)

LILY: Well, well, what have we here?!

HILDA: I made Mr. Lowe's favorite. Coffee mousse. I'll take those things away, Mr. Lowe. (*SHE sets the mousse down on a table, removes the muffin and salad from ARCHIE's tray and puts a dish of mousse in front of him.*) You've hardly eaten a thing, Miss Lily.

LILY: I have, too. I've finished my soup, and half my muffin and I will have my mousse. You can take my tray.

(HILDA takes LILY's tray, sets it aside and gives her the mousse. SHE then places ARCHIE's dishes on the tray and goes off to the kitchen. LILY and ARCHIE eat the mousse.)

LILY: This is good, isn't it? What's the matter, Archie? You've got to eat your mousse. You don't want to hurt Hilda's feelings. Do you?

(ARCHIE despondently takes another spoonful.)

LILY: It is good, isn't it?

(ARCHIE nods, sighs and sits staring into space. LILY continues to eat. HILDA reenters.)

HILDA: Is there anything wrong? I thought it turned out very good.

LILY: It's not your mousse, dear. Mr. Lowe is very depressed. He'll get over it. (*To ARCHIE.*) Shall we save your mousse for later dear?

(ARCHIE nods.)

LILY: Why don't you put Mr. Lowe's mousse in the refrigerator. He'll eat it tonight.

HILDA: Yes. Sure.

(HILDA takes ARCHIE's mousse and goes Off to the kitchen. FRITZ brings the walker in, as LILY finishes her mousse.)

LILY: That was good. Are you ready for your walk, Archie?

(HE shakes his head.)

LILY: Of course, you are. I do think I ought to wipe you off a little. Well, then do it yourself. (*SHE hands ARCHIE the napkin.*)

(HE wipes his face and shirt.)

LILY: There we are. Why don't you walk Mr. Lowe around the room, Fritz. Just ten minutes, that's all. Very slowly. (*SHE goes into the kitchen with her dessert dish and the napkin.*)

FRITZ: All ready, Mr. Lowe?

(ARCHIE shakes his head. FRITZ helps him out of the chair and onto the walker. ARCHIE moves about the room with great difficulty, almost falling a couple of times. HE stops.)

ARCHIE: Ahhh. Ahhh. Ahhba.

FRITZ: What's that, Mr. Lowe?

ARCHIE: Abba. (*HE points to his wheelchair.*)

FRITZ: Miss Lily said ten minutes. It's only three. Almost four.

(ARCHIE walks.)

FRITZ: I think if we go around the room it will be ten. You're doing good. We're almost there.

(The phone rings. LILY enters from the kitchen.)

LILY: I'll get it, Fritz. (*SHE picks up the phone.*) Hello? Yes, Myrtle. Could you hold it for a minute? (*SHE puts her hand over the receiver.*) I think that's enough, Fritz. Why don't we give Mr. Lowe his bath now. Here. I'll help you.

(LILY puts down the receiver and wheels the chair towards them. FRITZ helps ARCHIE into the chair.)

LILY: I'll bring down some fresh clothes.

FRITZ: Yes, Miss.

(HE wheels ARCHIE Off to the guest room.)

LILY: (*Picks up the phone.*) Yes. Myrtle. I'll take the call now. Hello? Yes, Oliver, I'm well, thank you. How are you? Well, we're home and Archie's doing as well as can be expected. No, he has improved. He has more movement and he can articulate a little more. It's going to be a long, slow process.

(ARCHIE, in the wheelchair, appears in the doorway, unseen by LILY.)

LILY: Oliver, no matter how much Archie improves it's very unlikely that he will ever act again. What *about* me? Oliver, we haven't appeared separately in over thirty years. I wouldn't even consider it. I don't care who you get. Of course, I miss the stage, but I can live without it. That's right. If Archie's career is over so is mine. I'm afraid you don't understand. No, I would not count on Archie, if I were you. I'm being perfectly honest with you. That's up to you. I'll tell him you called. No, I will not discuss it with Archie. The man is fighting for his very existence. Oliver, it is not a sacrifice. Oliver—.

(ARCHIE wheels himself back Off.)

LILY: I don't think that's wise. He tried to talk to Leslie before and it was very upsetting. I'll give him your love. Goodbye, Oliver. Goodbye!

(SHE hangs up and sits, greatly disturbed. HILDA enters from the kitchen.)

HILDA: Are you all right?

LILY: No.

HILDA: You mustn't drive yourself too hard. He's the one that's sick, not you, and if you get sick, you won't be any good to anyone.

LILY: I know that, Hilda.

HILDA: I think it's good that other people will be helping you.

LILY: I'll be all right, Hilda.

HILDA: Not if you don't take care of yourself. Maybe you ought to think of doing that play. I don't mean to interfere—.

LILY: Then don't!

HILDA: You know how restless you are when you're not in a play. You complain about your arthritis. You complain about this and you complain about that. You've been a different woman since you decided to go to work again.

LILY: I will not leave Mr. Lowe.

(FRITZ enters.)

FRITZ: He wants his soap.

LILY: Do we have anymore?

HILDA: I think there are a few bars left.

(FRITZ goes Off.)

HILDA: Fritz and I could look after Mr. Lowe. And we'll get all these people to help him with his speaking. After that, there won't be anything for you to do.

LILY: Except be here when he needs me.

HILDA: And what about all those hours of the day when you're not needed?

LILY: Hilda, I have no desire whatsoever to work without Archie.

HILDA: Are you so sure of that?

LILY: We made a pact, Mr. Lowe and I, over thirty years ago, that we would never appear on the stage without one another.

HILDA: That was before, Miss Lily.

LILY: Before what? I'd better get Fritz some fresh clothes. I'm going to lie down for a while. If anyone calls, just take the message.

(LILY goes Off. HILDA starts for the kitchen. The phone rings and SHE answers it.)

HILDA: Hello? Yes, Mr. Baxter, they're here. Mr. Lowe is taking a bath and Miss Lily is lying down. She asked me to take a message. He seems to be improving. That's what Miss Lily says. I don't know. I'm not a doctor, Mr. Baxter. I'll tell her you called. Yes. Yes, I wrote down your number.

(SHE hangs up as FRITZ enters with some clothes and a bar of soap.)

FRITZ: She looks very tired. What's the matter?

HILDA: Nothing.

(HE pats her shoulder and goes Off to the guest room. SHE starts for the kitchen and the phone rings again. SHE answers it.)

HILDA: Hello? Hello, Mr. Roger. I'm fine. They just came home a little while ago. Miss Lily is laying down and Mr. Lowe is taking a bath. Oh, I'm sure they'll be happy to see you. I'll tell them.

(FRITZ enters and motions for HILDA to hang up.)

HILDA: I have to go now, Mr. Roger. I'll tell them you called. Yes, yes . . . Goodbye, Mr. Roger. (*SHE hangs up.*) What is it?

FRITZ: He cut his wrist. No, don't wake her. Just call Dr. Miller. (*HE goes back Off.*)

HILDA: (*Picks up the phone and dials.*) Hello? Hello, Elsa. This is Hilda. Is the doctor in? I'm calling for Mrs. Lowe. Mr. Lowe's had an accident. Tell the doctor to come right over. As soon as he can. I don't know.

(The lights fade as SHE hangs up and goes Off to the guest room.)

END OF ACT II, SCENE 1

ACT II

Scene 2

(Dusk. Two months later. ARCHIE enters from the outside, using the walker. HE gets about with not too much difficulty. HE is followed by FRITZ, who closes the door behind them. FRITZ turns on several lamps. ARCHIE puts the walker aside and picks up a cane. . . . HE walks with a pronounced limp.)

ARCHIE: T—T—Tomorrow. Call—. (*HE can't think of the name.*)

FRITZ: Mr. Sedgewick.

ARCHIE: (*Nods.*) F—F—Fungus. P-P-Parasite. N-N-Not good.

FRITZ: Yes, sir.

ARCHIE: And—. Roof.

FRITZ: I'll tell Billy to take care of that, Mr. Lowe.

ARCHIE: B-B-Billy—.

FRITZ: I know. He's a lazy boy. But I'll get after him.

ARCHIE: Wh-Wh-What time—?

FRITZ: Five after six.

(ARCHIE shakes his head.)

FRITZ: You mean Miss Lily's train?

(ARCHIE nods.)

FRITZ: It leaves at eight o'clock. The same time as always, Mr. Lowe. The Chicago train always leaves at eight o'clock.

(ARCHIE nods impatiently.)

FRITZ: Would you like to watch some T.V., Mr. Lowe?

(ARCHIE shakes his head.)

FRITZ: How about a game of cards?

(ARCHIE shakes his head impatiently.)

ARCHIE: Lily!

FRITZ: She's probably upstairs, finishing her packing. Shall I tell her you want to speak to her?

ARCHIE: (*Shakes his head.*) S—S—S—S—. (*Pauses, then tries to think of another word.*) B-Book.

FRITZ: What book, Mr. Lowe?

ARCHIE: (*Shakes his head.*) Play.

FRITZ: Script?

(ARCHIE nods.)

FRITZ: What script, Mr. Lowe?

(ARCHIE thinks hard for a moment then points upstairs. HE points impatiently.)

ARCHIE: Play. Lily.

FRITZ: "Mountain Air"?

(ARCHIE nods.)

FRITZ: I don't know where you put it. Do you know where it is?

(ARCHIE shakes his head.)

FRITZ: Let's see. We were reading from it this afternoon. It should be around here somewhere. Here it is. Do you want to look at it?

(ARCHIE shakes his head and motions for FRITZ to lay it down.)

FRITZ: It'll be right here if you want to look at it later.

(ARCHIE nods impatiently.)

FRITZ: Do you want to play a game of checkers, Mr. Lowe?

(ARCHIE nods. . . . FRITZ goes to get the checkers.)

ARCHIE: Me! (*HE rises and gets the checkers then sets them down.*)

(FRITZ goes to help him.)

ARCHIE: No. Me!

(ARCHIE sets the board up, then picks up a red and black piece, conceals one in each hand, then offers his closed fists to FRITZ who points to one. ARCHIE opens his hand.)

ARCHIE: B-B-Black.

FRITZ: No, Mr. Lowe. That's red.

ARCHIE: (*HE nods.*) Black.

FRITZ: No, Mr. Lowe. You know what it is. That's right—.

ARCHIE: R-R-R-. Black.

(FRITZ shakes his head.)

ARCHIE: R-Red!

FRITZ: That's right.

ARCHIE: Red! Red, red, red.

(FRITZ moves and THEY start to play.)

ARCHIE: Ph—one?

FRITZ: No, Mr. Lowe. The phone didn't ring.

ARCHIE: Phone?

FRITZ: No, Mr. Lowe. The phone didn't *ring*.

ARCHIE: Nervous.

FRITZ: It's going to be all right. Hilda and me are here.

ARCHIE: I know.

(HILDA enters from the kitchen.)

HILDA: I put the coffee on, Mr. Lowe.

(ARCHIE nods and continues to concentrate on the game. HE looks about.)

FRITZ: What is it, Mr. Lowe?

ARCHIE: Play.

FRITZ: It's right over there, Mr. Lowe.

ARCHIE: Play.

(FRITZ rises and picks up the script, showing it to ARCHIE.)

FRITZ: It's right here, Mr. Lowe, whenever you want to look at it.

ARCHIE: (*Nods impatiently.*) Okay, okay.

HILDA: I'll see how Miss Lily is getting along with her packing. (*SHE goes upstairs.*)

FRITZ: Don't you want to play anymore, Mr. Lowe?

ARCHIE: Machine.

FRITZ: What machine?

ARCHIE: (*HE points to his mouth, then presses his finger down.*) Machine. Lily. (*HE points upstairs.*)

FRITZ: The dishwasher?

ARCHIE: Lily. Machine.

FRITZ: Miss Lily's machine?

(ARCHIE nods.)

FRITZ: Which machine is that? Oh, you don't mean her tape recorder, do you?

ARCHIE: (*Nods.*) Tape. Tape.

FRITZ: What about it?

ARCHIE: Me.

FRITZ: You want it?

(ARCHIE nods.)

FRITZ: Now?

ARCHIE: (*Shakes his head.*) Leave it. Leave it here. Tell her—leave it here.

FRITZ: I'll tell her, Mr. Lowe. You can tell her yourself. I'll remind you.

ARCHIE: Forget!

FRITZ: No, no. I won't forget.

ARCHIE: Important.

FRITZ: I'm sure she won't take it with her. It's part of your lessons.

ARCHIE: (*Nods.*) I know. I know. Her lesson, too.

FRITZ: We'll remind her. She can buy another one in Chicago.

(The phone rings. LILY enters from upstairs. SHE is wearing a suit that SHE travels in—, Chanel, perhaps.)

LILY: I'll get it, Fritz. (*SHE picks up the phone.*) Hello? Yes, Mrs. Donaldson. I see. I see. Yes. Yes, of course. I understand. Don't worry about it. We'll get someone else. Let's see. What time were you down for? (*SHE picks up a pad.*) Yes. Here you are. Eleven o'clock. How long will you be away? Just a minute. I want to make a note of it. (*SHE picks up a pencil and writes on the pad.*) Why don't you give us a ring when you get back? And thank you so much. Yes. Yes, of course, I will. Thank you, Mrs. Donaldson.

(SHE hangs up, looks up a number in the back of the pad, then dials. ARCHIE has gone back to the game.)

LILY: Did you enjoy your walk, dear?

(ARCHIE nods.)

LILY: Mrs. Donaldson will be out of town for a week. I've got to find a replacement. She works with you at eleven o'clock. (*SHE hangs up, looks up another number and dials.*) Hello? Hello, Jimmy. Is your mother in? I see. What time will she be back? This is Mrs. Lowe. Would you ask her to call me when she gets in? Thank you, dear. (*SHE hangs up.*) I know I've forgotten something. I can't think of what it is.

ARCHIE: Tape, Machine.

LILY: I'm leaving that here for you. It's right here on the table. Yes, dear? What is it?

ARCHIE: Tape.

LILY: Cassettes?

(ARCHIE nods.)

LILY: I've got a whole supply. They're right here in this drawer.

ARCHIE: Kk—K—KK. Caps.

LILY: Cassettes.

ARCHIE: S-Set. Cap. Set.

LILY: Cassettes.

ARCHIE: Capsettes.

LILY: Cassettes.

ARCHIE: Capsettes.

LILY: That's pretty good.

FRITZ: Do you want to play with Mr. Lowe?

LILY: No, that's all right. Is there anything you want me to do, Archie, before I leave?

(ARCHIE shakes his head.)

LILY: I feel like I'm stepping into the lion's den.

ARCHIE: Don't—worry.

LILY: That's easy for you to say.

ARCHIE: No.

LILY: I think this is a big mistake. Suppose I fall flat on my face?

ARCHIE: Don't worry.

LILY: I expect you to be there for the previews.

ARCHIE: I—will.

LILY: Taking notes.

ARCHIE: The—b-b-best I can. Don't—upstage.

LILY: I'll be happy if I can get my lines out.

ARCHIE: No—tricks.

LILY: Really, Archie!

ARCHIE: Give—Roger—.

LILY: What?

ARCHIE: Chance.

LILY: Really? Is that who you're concerned about? Roger?

ARCHIE: You—can—take care of—yourself.

LILY: I'm glad you're so confident. I hope you realize that I'm doing this only because you want me to.

ARCHIE: I know.

LILY: Will you be up to coming to Chicago?

(ARCHIE nods.)

LILY: It's only five weeks from now.

ARCHIE: I will.

LILY: You don't have to be at every preview. If it does not go well in Chicago I told Oliver that I am stepping out.

(HILDA enters.)

HILDA: Would you like some coffee, Miss Lily? I just made a fresh pot and Mr. Lowe is having some.

LILY: Not really.

HILDA: Would you like some tea?

LILY: Well, maybe just half a cup.

(HILDA goes into the kitchen.)

FRITZ: I'll give Hilda some help.

ARCHIE: No, no. I will.

LILY: That's really not necessary, Archie.

ARCHIE: I want to.

(HE starts to pick up his cane, changes his mind and limps into the kitchen.)

LILY: He's doing very well, isn't he?

FRITZ: Very well.

LILY: I plan to speak to Mr. Lowe every morning, but I would like to talk to you and Hilda at night, after Mr. Lowe has gone to bed. . . .

FRITZ: Certainly. You mustn't worry, Miss Lily. We can take care of Mr. Lowe.

(HILDA enters with coffee things on a tray.)

LILY: That's very thoughtful of you, Hilda.

(As HILDA sets down the tray ARCHIE enters with a cake. HE walks very carefully, stumbling slightly just once.)

HILDA: Mr. Lowe baked that himself.

ARCHIE: (*Sets down the cake and points to HILDA.*) Helped.

HILDA: I hardly did anything.

ARCHIE: Helped.

LILY: It's lovely, Archie.

ARCHIE: R-Read.

LILY: "Bon Chance." "Chance" is feminine, dear. It should be "Bonne Chance."

ARCHIE: Eat!

HILDA: I'll get some plates.

LILY: Please. You and Fritz must have some, too. I insist.

HILDA: Thank you. (*SHE goes into the kitchen.*)

ARCHIE: Surprised?

LILY: Of course, I'm not surprised. You'll use any excuse to bake a cake.

ARCHIE: Simple layer cake. First thing—since—stroke.

LILY: It looks good.

ARCHIE: Maybe not—moist.

(HILDA reenters with plates and utensils.)

HILDA: Would you like me to cut the cake, Mr. Lowe?

ARCHIE: No. (*HE takes the knife and cuts the cake.*)

LILY: It looks delicious.

ARCHIE: Not—moist.

LILY: It feels moist. Won't you have some coffee, Hilda. Fritz?

FRITZ: (*Nods.*) Thank you.

(HILDA goes into the kitchen and reenters with two cups, then serves the coffee. LILY tastes the cake.)

ARCHIE: Wh—What do you—think?

LILY: I think it's fine. What do *you* think?

ARCHIE: (*Tastes cake.*) Not bad.

HILDA: It's very good, Mr. Lowe.

ARCHIE: What do you think—Fritz?

FRITZ: Very good.

(THEY proceed to eat.)

LILY: By the way, Hilda, Mrs. Donaldson called. She'll be out of town for about a week. We'll have to find somebody to replace her.

HILDA: What about Mary Johnson?

LILY: I gave her a call but she was out. I left a message for her to call us.

HILDA: Don't worry, Miss Lily. I'll take care of it.

LILY: Mr. Lowe is scheduled to see the doctor next week.

HILDA: I know. We have it marked down.

ARCHIE: You worry—about—your—. Your—.

LILY: Performance.

ARCHIE: Per—mance.

LILY: Per—for—mance.

ARCHIE: For—mance.

LILY: Performance.

ARCHIE: Formance.

LILY: Yes, dear.

ARCHIE: You'll—be—fine. Eat.

LILY: It's delicious, dear. It really is. But I'm much too nervous to eat. Besides, that piece is much too big for me.

ARCHIE: Take—rest for Roger.

LILY: Roger is much too fat as it is.

ARCHIE: Later—diet.

LILY: Yes, he does love your cooking.

HILDA: I'll wrap up the rest of the cake.

LILY: What time is it?

FRITZ: A quarter to seven. We should leave in half an hour. I'll bring down your bag, Miss Lily.

ARCHIE: More?

FRITZ: No thank you, Mr. Lowe. That was fine. (*HE goes upstairs.*)

ARCHIE: (*Rises.*) Scuse.

LILY: Where are you going, dear?

ARCHIE: Bathroom. (*HE starts Off, weaves slightly, goes back for his cane and goes Off to the Guest Room.*)

LILY: That's the fifth time today. Do you think he's all right?

HILDA: I think the improvement is a miracle.

LILY: The doctor said it might be rapid at first, but then it would slow down.

HILDA: He'll be well again.

LILY: Up to a point. He'll never act again, Hilda.

HILDA: He can do other things.

LILY: He's an excellent director. I don't want to go. Why is he so anxious for me to leave?

HILDA: You will be closer to him acting in a play than you will be staying here, Miss Lily. Besides—.

LILY: Besides—what?

HILDA: The day comes, sometimes, when we must go alone.

LILY: I don't know what you mean.

HILDA: It's just that—well—I think he wants you to get used to the idea that you may not always be together all the time.

LILY: Mr. Jeffries wants to name a theatre after us. In New York, that is. I'm not particularly anxious for some building to bear my name—cold bricks and a marquee. A newly decorated theatre. I was trained by Ellen Terry, you know. Do you know who Ellen Terry was?

(HILDA shakes her head.)

LILY: Not many people do. She was a great lady and a great artist—and a woman to the very end—which was sometimes embarrassing to her friends. The first time I met Mr. Lowe he fell flat on his face. It was backstage of course. I asked to be introduced to him. When Archie and I perform there's electricity in the air. It's always been that way—from the very beginning.

(FRITZ enters with LILY's bag.)

FRITZ: I'll put your suitcase in the car, Miss Lily.

LILY: Thank you, Fritz.

(HE goes out the front door with the bag.)

LILY: He will lead a normal life. He must!

HILDA: He will, Miss Lily. He's almost there already. I'll wrap that cake up for you.

(HILDA takes the cake dishes and the cake and goes Off to the kitchen with the tray. LILY sits lost in thought. ARCHIE enters and sits beside her. HE clears the checker board, picks up a red and black piece and extends them within closed fists toward her.)

LILY: What, dear? Oh, I'm sorry. (*SHE points to one of ARCHIE's hands.*)

ARCHIE: R—Red.

LILY: So it is.

(ARCHIE sets up the board and waits for LILY to play. SHE is far away.)

ARCHIE: You!

LILY: Oh. Yes. Yes, of course.

ARCHIE: You—don't—play?

LILY: I guess I'm not up to it really.

ARCHIE: You—talk?

LILY: What do you want to talk about?

ARCHIE: You—*want*—talk?

LILY: Not necessarily. We've never really needed words, have we?

(HE shakes his head.)

LILY: Oh, my darling—.

ARCHIE: No—crying. Stage!

LILY: Yes. I shall save my tears for the stage.

ARCHIE: Good—enough—for both—of us.

LILY: That's a tall order, isn't it?

ARCHIE: You—do it.

LILY: I'm glad you're so confident.

(The phone rings and LILY answers it.)

LILY: Hello? Hello Mary. I'm fine. Yes, Mr. Lowe is coming along very well. I was wondering if you were free tomorrow. Eleven o'clock. I see. Maybe I can switch with someone. Gladys is free all day. Can we count on you for —. (*SHE consults the pad.*) Three o'clock. Fine. If you don't hear from us we'll expect you at three. Thank you, dear. Yes. Yes, thank you. (*SHE hangs up, looks up a number and dials.*) Oh, dear. No one is ever home when you want them! (*SHE hangs up.*)

ARCHIE: Sit. Hilda.

LILY: I'll feel much better if I know your schedule is covered.

ARCHIE: Sit! Hilda!

LILY: I won't sleep all night.

(ARCHIE rises, takes his cane and starts for the Guest Room.)

LILY: Where are you going?

ARCHIE: Bathroom!

LILY: You've just been to the bathroom.

(HE goes Off. FRITZ enters from the outside.)

FRITZ: The car is ready, Miss Lily.

LILY: We've still got time, haven't we?

FRITZ: Oh, yes.

(HILDA enters from the kitchen and clears the rest of the dishes.)

HILDA: (*To Fritz.*) You can help me with the dishes. (*SHE goes into the kitchen.*)

FRITZ: Yes, Ma'am.

(FRITZ winks at LILY and follows HILDA into the kitchen. LILY picks up the phone and dials. ARCHIE reenters.)

LILY: Why do you keep going to the bathroom?

ARCHIE: Nervous.

LILY: What have you got to be nervous about? I'm the one that's going to be up on that stage all by myself.

(HE shakes his head.)

LILY: What do you mean "no"?

(HE points to himself.)

LILY: In spirit maybe.

ARCHIE: Sit down!

(LILY hangs up and sits.)

ARCHIE: Play!

(SHE sighs and moves a checker. THEY play in silence. The game picks up speed.)

ARCHIE: I win! Another. I'll—take black. You—take red.

(THEY set up the board. The phone rings. ARCHIE rises and picks it up.)

ARCHIE: Hello? (*HE struggles with word.*) Minute. (*To LILY.*) It's—for you.

LILY: Thank you. (*SHE takes the phone.*) Hello? Yes, Ingrid. Yes, that was he. I see. Yes. Yes, of course. Well, why don't you wait and see how you feel in the morning? No. No. I'll be gone. You can talk to Hilda. Thank you. Thank you, Ingrid. (*SHE hangs up.*) Ingrid has a cold and she doesn't want to give it to you.

ARCHIE: What time?

LILY: Two o'clock.

ARCHIE: (*Picks up schedule and studies it for a moment, then sets it down.*) Tomorrow. (*Points to himself.*) Me! Hilda. Don't worry!

LILY: I will too worry and there's no use pretending that I won't. Half of me will be up on that stage and the other half will be right here in this room with you, and so help me God, if you don't improve by leaps and bounds I am coming right back. I mean it. (*SHE goes to the kitchen doorway.*) Fritz, I think we ought to be starting, don't you.

(FRITZ enters from the kitchen.)

LILY: (*To ARCHIE.*) I'll call you in the morning.

(HILDA enters and SHE and LILY embrace.)

LILY: Goodbye, Hilda.

HILDA: Good luck, Miss Lily.

LILY: Thank you, dear. (*SHE goes to ARCHIE and kisses him perfunctorily, almost harshly.*) Come along, Fritz.

(LILY starts Off, FRITZ precedes her Off. SHE stops in the doorway.)

LILY: Oh, Ingrid Donovan called. She has a cold. She'll call you in the morning. (*HILDA nods. LILY hesitates for a moment and then goes Off.*)

HILDA: Well, she's gone.

(ARCHIE heaves a sigh.)

HILDA: Would you like to play a game of checkers?

(ARCHIE shakes his head.)

HILDA: (*A little sharply, SHE wants him to speak*). What was that?

ARCHIE: No!

HILDA: If you need me, I'll be in the kitchen.

ARCHIE: Yes!

(HILDA goes off to the kitchen. ARCHIE goes to checker game and slowly folds the board, placing the checkers in the box. HE sits and sighs. There is a long pause. HE starts to pick up the tape recorder but stops as HILDA reenters.)

HILDA: Is there anything you want, Mr. Lowe?

ARCHIE: No—thank you.

HILDA: I'll be in my room.

(HILDA goes off. ARCHIE waits to make sure SHE's gone, then picks up the tape recorder. LILY reenters and stands watching him. HE almost drops the recorder and LILY starts to move towards him but stops herself in time. ARCHIE sits thinking, then presses the record button.)

ARCHIE: I was—born—in Wisconsin—

(LILY smiles and tiptoes off.)

ARCHIE: and I've always been a farmer at heart.

CURTAIN

INSIDE

A Play in One Act

CAST OF CHARACTERS

Librarian
Boy
Young Man
Little Girl
First Girl
Second Girl
Soldier

SCENE

A library.

(The people in this play do not talk; they think out loud. We are aware of two spheres of action. One consists of the physical action of the characters and is designated by pantomime, the other is that of the mind and is created by the spoken words.

Since it is early afternoon on a warm summer day and the sun is bright and gold, there is a pleasant glowing light in the library. The light, filtered by the ivy on the outside of the building, comes from the window on the right, the one on the left, and the three in the rear. It falls on the highly polished table near the reference books and magazines, left front, on the LIBRARIAN's desk, right front, and on the card file in the center of the room. All the woodwork is well shellacked and shiny, including the bench (in front of the card file) whose back so rudely faces the audience. However, in the rear, between the bookshelves, whose ends face us, the light is dimmer—dusky—and the red, green, and brown covers of the straightly arranged books take on a deeper and richer color. There are colored pictures on the pinboards, placed at the end of each bookcase. There is a vase of yellow and orange flowers on the LIBRARIAN's desk. The atmosphere is cool and refreshing, yet has a slight air of mustiness about it. Time, if it moves at all, ticks very slowly.

When the curtain rises, there are three people on stage. A high-school BOY is thumbing through books in the novel section. At the table is a YOUNG MAN of about twenty-one. HE is handsome, tall and slim, with soft blue eyes, thin, small nose, and long wavy black hair. His sport shirt has a patch in the back, and the seat of his trousers is shiny. There is a pile of books in front of him. HE is leaning back comfortably in a chair, looking through one of them, reading slowly and searchingly. HE comes to a line that intrigues him, looks up thoughtfully, putting one leg over the arm of the chair, and gazes into space. HE twists around, leans far back, and smiles.

The LIBRARIAN is a woman of forty, medium height, and good figure. SHE is dark complexioned and her black eyes have an intelligent, piercing look. Her hair is turning gray and is the only messy thing about her. SHE probably combs it before going to work, but sticking a pencil behind her ear every other minute, or scratching her head when thinking doesn't help to keep it in place. Her movements are quick, almost sudden, and efficient. Her speaking voice would be dry and brittle, and most of her remarks sarcastic. However, her thought voice is not bitter, and once in a while it is even soft and young. Her mind has not completely taken over her outward appearance and probably never will. SHE is too intelligent, and too full of good literature not to appreciate the good SHE does find. SHE is at her desk now, arranging a bunch of cards. Every once in a while her eyes glance up at the YOUNG MAN.)

LIBRARIAN: (*SHE is looking at the YOUNG MAN at the table.*) Well, have you found it yet? Yes, I mean you with the patched polo shirt, and lovely long lashes. (*SHE snaps an elastic band about some cards and lays them aside.*) You've been searching long enough. Day in, day out, you sit there and squirm. If you want to know something, why don't you ask me? Librarians know everything. (*SHE takes the pencil from her ear, checks a card, and puts it behind the other ear.*) Don't you have a job? How are you going to earn your bread? (*Recalling.*) "By the sweat of thy brow, by the sweat of thy brow."

BOY: (*Reading from a book.*) "He closed the door behind him. 'Anne,' he said softly, 'did you mean it?' Anne turned to him; she was breathing heavily. Her eyes were warm and compelling, and he felt the warmth all over. Slowly, he walked towards her. She remained perfectly still. Suddenly, he had her in his arms, his lips sought her lips, and his hand was on her thigh." (*Disgustedly.*) The end of the chapter. (*HE slams the book closed and replaces it, looking for another one.*)

LIBRARIAN: There's nothing out that window except the lawn. Perhaps you'd like to cut the grass. Cut the grass every noon for a week, and you could earn enough to buy some decent clothes. (*SHE reaches around for the phone, and dials a number.*) This is a beautiful library. Nicer than the Roxbury branch, the Krevis branch, or even the main branch. None of them have our lovely flowers. (*SHE talks on the phone. Now SHE is listening.*) Myrtle is clumsy. Fat, clumsy, and inefficient. (*SHE talks again, hangs up, and returns to the cards.*) Are you still searching? The books are heavy and their number so large. There are so many pages, and the print is so fine.

YOUNG MAN: (*HE turns from the window and is reading* The Moon and Sixpence *by Somerset Maugham.*) "Beauty is something wonderful and strange that the artist fashions out of the chaos of the world in the torment of his soul. And when he has made it, it is not given to all to know it." Hm. Yes. Yet I know the wind and the blue sky, without torment. I know breathing, and that is not torment. (*HE rises and walks to the rear, looking out of one of the back windows.*)

LIBRARIAN: (*Picks up a book from the desk.*) When did this get in? I haven't spoken to him yet. He's been coming here every day, and he hasn't said a word to me. Maybe if I offered him this—new, hard to get, five cents a day at a lending library. He would look up at me and smile very gratefully. "Oh. Thanks ever so much." (*Looks at table.*) I'll give it—. Gone! Now where have you gone? You make me nervous. What is he looking for?

BOY: (*Reading from a book.*) "Pepita lay naked on the bamboo cot. The setting sun, shining through the walls of the bamboo hut made strange patterns on her smooth, brown skin. She was half asleep when she heard Arturo's heavy footsteps in the doorway. Pepita pretended she didn't know he was there as he took off his clothes, and threw them onto the chair. She felt something warm at her side. It was Arturo. She slid over and her—." Wow!

(*HE folds the edge of the page down, looking first to see if anyone is watching, and closes the book, putting it under his left arm.*)

LIBRARIAN: (*Watching the YOUNG MAN.*) Do you plan to comb every volume, every line, every thought? There's a lot been said, my man, most of it humbug. Words and thoughts, words and thoughts. What are they? Just words and thoughts.

YOUNG MAN: (*HE is walking back to his seat with a couple of more books.*) "Atoms. All matter is composed of atoms. These minute, elementary particles are always in motion, and are the basis for the structure of all substances." I am composed of atoms, and they're always in motion. (*HE looks at his hand and feels it. HE looks at the book and feels it. HE feels the air.*) "Atoms are composed of even smaller particles, electrons, protons, and neutrons—positive, negative, and neutral, moving in fixed orbits." Is that desk in constant motion? Our sight is so limited. Even our eyeballs are atoms. Think of it. Just think of it. How strange things really are. (*HE walks quickly to the table, and writes down something. HE sits down and thumbs rapidly through the book HE just took from the shelves.*)

LIBRARIAN: More books. I'll have to put them back. He has so many books that it would look silly to bring him another. If I did get to know him I probably wouldn't be able to get rid of him—. Would tell me everything about everything with a sickening enthusiasm. He looks so happy.

YOUNG MAN: (*HE slumps down in the chair, and with his hands investigates his face. HE feels his chin and jaw bone.*) Bone. Skin. (*Prods the hollows of his cheeks and his cheek bones. Feels his nose.*) Nostrils. Life breath. Eyelashes. Forehead. (*Taps his skull, and encases the top of his head in his two hands.*) Hard skull. (*Smiles and then jumps up in his seat and continues looking through the books.*)

LIBRARIAN: (*SHE picks up the book and goes toward the table.*) How many times have I walked across this floor? It's a good floor, solid linoleum, yet soft.

(SHE walks to the YOUNG MAN, who looks up and smiles at her. SHE gives him the book, and HE thanks her. SHE speaks to him rapidly, friendly, and nervously, and HE replies.)

LIBRARIAN: Go back to your desk now old woman. That's enough. (*SHE finishes speaking to the YOUNG MAN and walks to the catalogue, pretending to look up something.*) You're a fool, an old fool. He was so polite.

YOUNG MAN: What made her do that? It was friendly of her. Maybe she's disappointed that I haven't checked out any books. I'll take this one she gave me. What is it? Hm. Never heard of it. Probably some new, popular trash.

LIBRARIAN: He didn't want the book. Of course not. He's a thinker, can't you see? What do you think of, thinker?

(Walks to desk, and sits, looking and thinking. The SISTER of the BOY comes up the stairs and enters center stage, her back to the audience. [This is the only entrance or exit.] SHE is twelve years old and a little dirty. SHE walks very slowly and looks about with wondering eyes.)

LITTLE GIRL: So this is the adult library. How shiny the bench is, and the table and desk. It's very dignified this place is. (*SHE stands at the bench.*)

LIBRARIAN: (*SHE is still thinking and her elbows are on the desk.*) Dirty little brat.

LITTLE GIRL: But it's so quiet in here. It's so heavy. Is someone dead? You want to whisper and cry. Maybe it's sad because it's the grown-up library.

LIBRARIAN: Don't they ever wash, these scrawny little girls in cotton rags with knotted hair, and snotty noses?

LITTLE GIRL: (*Walks in and sits on bench, her back still to the audience.*) This wood is so smooth. Look at that man, studying so hard. He must have a lot of homework, poor man. Why are they so quiet? There are no kids laughing here, and no little boys running between the bookshelves. There's not even a long line to wait in to check books out.

LIBRARIAN: (*SHE is now checking cards again.*) Look at that face, will you? You would think parents would take some pride in their offspring. Why do people have to be squawling brats first? Why do we have to be giggling, gossiping girls before we become civilized, intelligent adults?

LITTLE GIRL: That librarian looks so cross. They're so much nicer in the children's room, though there are some mean ones. There aren't even any big drawings on the wall. I wonder where brother is. I don't see him.

> *(SHE looks about, sees him, jumps up, waves to him and starts to run. This is just what the LIBRARIAN has waited for. SHE stands in front of the LITTLE GIRL, drilling her with her eyes and telling her that SHE'd better keep quiet. The YOUNG MAN is watching them.)*

LIBRARIAN: Ought to wring her little neck. Have to be taught manners, just like a puppy. He's still at it, isn't he?

LITTLE GIRL: (*Tiptoes to her BROTHER, who takes no notice of her, after seeing SHE is present.*) Old meanie. She's so mean.

> *(The YOUNG MAN suddenly bursts out laughing—silently, of course. HE leans back and laughs.)*

LIBRARIAN: I think he's going crazy. He's so happy. What's he looking for?

BOY: What's the name of that book that Inkie told me about, with that good part? I can't remember. Let's see. (*HE searches for the book.*)

LITTLE GIRL: How solemn the books are. But they look good. (*SHE picks up books here and there.*) Lots of big books with little print.

They look exciting. So many interesting things to read. But they don't have any pictures at all. It would be nice if they had just one nice picture in the front of every one.

BOY: It was about a kid in the slums. It was—. Oh, what was the name of it? I could ask the librarian.

LITTLE GIRL: How nice they smell. They must have millions of far-away pictures in them. England long ago, French adventure stories, old German festivals. I must take this smell home with me. Brother shall take out a book for me.

> *(SHE pulls the BOY's shirt and HE looks down at her. SHE asks him a question to which HE gives a careless nod, and resumes his search.)*

LITTLE GIRL: I'll get the beach chair out on the porch, and I'll have mother make me some lemonade, and then I'll sit all afternoon and read.

BOY: If I asked her, she'd probably know what I was looking for. I'd feel funny.

LITTLE GIRL: This looks like a wonderful book, *The Last Puritan*, by George San-tay-ana. I'll take it. (*SHE places it under her arm, and begins to wander about, looking at everything.*)

LIBRARIAN: How I hate those noisy, running brats. They come in here, and in two minutes the place is a madhouse. And when you tell them to be quiet, they look so surprised.

BOY: Oh, I'll ask her. How could she know?

> *(HE goes to the desk and speaks to the LIBRARIAN, who takes him to the catalogue, and looks through the cards.)*

LIBRARIAN: I know perfectly well why you want that book. Chapter sixteen, or seventeen, isn't it? Greasy young boys with pimpled faces. (*SHE takes him to the bookshelves.*) We ought to make a special list for them, just like we print lists of historical novels, or scientific books. Novels with sexy, pardon me, in their language it's dirty parts, guaranteed to satisfy, approved by the high school principal and board of education. (*SHE hands the book to the BOY and goes back to her desk.*)

LITTLE GIRL: How beautiful the flowers are. What kind are they? Mrs. Henry told us in class the other day. We have no flowers in the children's room. They smell just like mother's perfume.

BOY: Of course, she didn't know. You should have asked her before. (*HE opens the book and looks through it carefully.*) Now, let's see—.

LIBRARIAN: (*Watching the YOUNG MAN.*) Tell me, thinker, have you set a time limit on your research, or is it a life work? No, he doesn't seem to be in a hurry. Does he think his answer is there, waiting for him? How mistaken he is! How disappointed he'll be.

LITTLE GIRL: (*SHE's looking at the pictures on the pin boards on the ends of each bookcase.*) This is a picture of a ballet dancer. How white and fluffy her dress is. Maybe I can be a beautiful ballet dancer, when I grow up. Oh, but her face is all painted. Her eyebrows are so black and her mouth so red. I shall be a dancer with no bright paint.

YOUNG MAN: The sweetest time is night time. The most expressive thing in the world is a breeze. Night air and cool breezes are a poem.

LITTLE GIRL: The man dancer has a pretty costume. If it weren't bright blue, if it were red, it would look like long underwear. Doesn't it itch him? If it does, he controls himself very well, because he smiles so nicely. (*As SHE backs away from the picture SHE twirls about slightly. If SHE were at home, SHE would be dancing about the room.*)

BOY: Is this the right book? I can't seem to find it. (*HE is still thumbing through the same book.*)

LIBRARIAN: I wonder how many notes I would have if I started taking them when I was his age. (*SHE gets up from the desk and puts some books on the shelf.*) Haven't you found that chapter yet, boy? It's sixteen, pimpled face, chapter sixteen. I wouldn't be surprised if you came and asked me to help you find it.

(Two HIGH SCHOOL GIRLS come running up the steps. THEY have their arms full of school books. The FIRST GIRL is prettier than the SECOND GIRL, but THEY are both attractive, young and healthy. THEY glance about the room, and after consulting

each other THEY make for the table, sitting opposite the YOUNG MAN.)

FIRST GIRL: French Revolution, Reign of Terror, assignats, Bony-party—. Why did I have to take that rotten course!? (*Opens book.*) Oh, my. Fifteen pages—twenty years to outline.

SECOND GIRL: (*Looking at LIBRARIAN.*) Old Crosspot is still growling. Doesn't she ever smile?

(Every once in a while the GIRLS put their heads together and chatter, in pantomime, of course. This occurs all through their speeches and their time on stage. The SECOND GIRL leans over and tells something to the FIRST GIRL, who looks at the LIBRARIAN.)

SECOND GIRL: I wonder how old she is, and if she ever had any boyfriends.

FIRST GIRL: That's a nice dress Crosspot has on today. Maybe she has a date with an encyclopedia. (*SHE notices the YOUNG MAN.*) Well, look what we have here! Where have you been all my life, honey chile?

(SHE leans over to the SECOND GIRL and begins babbling. The LIBRARIAN starts over toward them.)

FIRST GIRL: Oh, oh. Now we're in for it.

LIBRARIAN: Why have you stopped giggling? I haven't said anything—yet.

(SHE tells them that they're high school students and ought to act like ones, and not like a child of that age over there. The GIRLS nod sweetly and apologetically, and return to their books.)

FIRST GIRL: I'd like to crown her with that vase of flowers. (*Mimicking.*) You're high school students now and ought to act like ones. What are we supposed to do? Take a pose and hold it?

LITTLE GIRL: (*SHE is looking at her book, and sniffs at it once in a while.*) What is that strong smell? Is it the paper? It's not the ink. It's not the cover. Maybe it's the glue.

LIBRARIAN: I have to keep them quiet. In a few years they'll be mature. Will I get any benefit from it? No. Probably won't see them any more. But I have to keep them quiet.

FIRST GIRL: (*SHE smiles at the YOUNG MAN.*) Honey, you're a dream.

(SHE leans over and asks him something. Very formally and politely. HE hands her an eraser.)

FIRST GIRL: Pretty good sister. You're a very smooth article. (*SHE smiles and hands it back to him.*)

SECOND GIRL: Flirting? She has the mind of a grasshopper. Can't she see he's busy, really busy? There's a time for such things. She must think she's very pretty. Well, she is, isn't she? Yes.

YOUNG MAN: Eraser. I'd like to give you more than an eraser. What soft swelling young breasts. They're so much nicer when they're just forming. Young sweetness. Make a beautiful painting of them. (*HE leans back in his chair.*) "A thing of beauty is a joy forever. Its loveliness increases; . . ."

(*HE bursts out laughing—silently. The LIBRARIAN and the GIRLS look at him, but HE doesn't notice them.*)

YOUNG MAN: "It will never pass into nothingness." Hm, won't it? (*HE looks down at the floor in thought. Then HE looks at the ceiling.*)

BOY: I know this is the right book. Now where is that chapter? (*Reading.*) "Mollie was sad that—." No.

LIBRARIAN: (*Looking at the GIRLS.*) I see you've noticed him, too. I wonder if you'll be able to find out what he's doing. You probably wouldn't understand, if you did.

SECOND GIRL: She thinks he's good-looking. Good-looking? He's beautiful. Long, tapering fingers—so sensitive. His hair is so dark and shiny. Look at that wave in the front. Forehead, small and white with one wrinkle in the center. Eyebrows so delicately curved—like a woman's—and those long lashes.

LIBRARIAN: (*SHE is putting books on the shelf.*) Books, books—. How many I've read; how many I've put on the shelf. Which is the true world now? Mine is so unreal, like a dream. The other is down in black and white.

SECOND GIRL: His eyes are so deep and blue. I wish I could get close and look into them, and through them, and behind them. His skin is so smooth. He couldn't be shaving. Wait a minute. Yes, he does. Thin nose. Nostrils so fine you can see them move when he breathes. Finely curved full lips. How I'd like to feel them press against mine—. And those fine sensitive hands on my neck. He must have a hard, clean body. (*SHE erases something. Coughs.*) Sex. I always thought it meant a man's hairy, smelly body pressing against you. But he is smooth and beautiful, and I could love him, and he would make everything good. How fine his neck rises from his chest and supports his head.

FIRST GIRL: How wonderful it will be to be free from school, free to do what you want. Time is yours and no one stands over it, and slices it up and hands you pieces of it at a time.

LITTLE GIRL: This place will be even quieter at night, when everyone is gone. It won't be all dark, except in some of the corners. (*SHE sits down on the edge of the bench, watching the LIBRARIAN.*) The moon will shine through the window, and throw the shadow of the window pane on the desk and on the floor. The flowers will be all closed up—Mrs. Henry said so—and the clock will tick loudly because there won't be another sound. If the window is open maybe the wind will rustle the papers on the desk, and blow ripples on the ink in the bottle. The books will be all alone on the shelf, and the tables will be empty, and nobody will be sitting in the chairs. They'll be cold and stiff. The shadow of the window will crawl inch by inch across the floor and over the catalogue, and up the wall, and soon it will fade because it will get lighter and lighter. Then the sun will come up and it will be really light. The librarian will be in bed, and her hair will be all mussed up, and her eyes closed. Soon she'll get up, and her eyes won't be cross 'cause there won't be anyone there to be cross at. Then she'll drink coffee, and eat toast, and come to work. The library will be all lit up by then, and when she unlocks the door, she'll bring life into the room again. She'll throw out the old flowers and put newer and prettier ones in, and she'll stick her pencil in her hair, and then I'll come in the door, and then she'll be cross again, and now we begin again and I'm sitting on the bench, waiting for brother.

BOY: If I don't find that chapter soon—. (*Reading.*) "Mollie was that kind of a girl. All the guys on the block said so, and they knew. So Ben wasn't surprised one night on his way home from the new job, when he saw a pair of shapely gams—."

SECOND GIRL: I wonder if the man I marry will be as beautiful as he is. No. No such luck. He'll probably have a pot belly like uncle. If I went up to you and said, "I love you and would make you a wonderful wife," would you smile at me, and kiss me, or run as fast as you could?

YOUNG MAN: Could I be dead? I can't see how. What's in me now could never die. That yearning and aching and love could never die. Maybe I as an individual—no, not even that could not exist. You have lived forever, and will live forever. But you agree her breasts will some day be dust? Yes. Well, don't you think you're made of flesh, too? Sometimes I wonder. Now, come, come. Are you a God, or something? Now, you've said something. I might be a God. Who is to say? God? Don't make me laugh.

LIBRARIAN: Maybe he knows what is real and what is fanciful. Is that what you're searching for? If it is, I'll tell you what you'll find. Nothing! No answer at all. You'll never know. And stop smiling. Cheerful, happy ass.

BOY: (*Reading.*) "Ben wasn't dumb. When he opened that door he knew what was flying. Mollie had on a thin, lace negligee. Macy's basement, $2.95. Ben slammed the door, and strode into the room. 'Make yourself at home,' Mollie drawled drily."

FIRST GIRL: I wish this term were over and summer were here. Then I'd be stretched out on the hot gritty sand in my new, white lastex. Not many men around, but there must be some sailors or soldiers around the beach. Every time you see them, they're on furlough.

LITTLE GIRL: Isn't it funny, how you get used to this quiet? Are they still running around and making a lot of noise and messing up the shelves in the children's room?

BOY: (*Reading.*) " 'Make yourself comfortable, big boy,' Mollie added meaningly. As he sat down she came over to him. 'You've grown up,' she whispered. 'So have you,' he managed to stammer, proud that he had a comeback. She put her arms about his neck, and he felt her warm breath on his cheek. His pulse beat wildly. This is it." (*HE stops reading, and looks up.*) This is it all right. (*HE closes the book, and walks to the desk.*)

LIBRARIAN: (*Checking his books out.*) Well, I see you've found it. Too bad you can't ask me. I could help a lot in your search for good literature. Hmph!

BOY: Why did I hesitate in asking her? How could she know? Furthest thing from her mind.

LITTLE GIRL: Some time I will come here all the time, and maybe forget about the children's room. I shall be quiet and comfortable here, and very dignified, and maybe wear a silk dress, like the librarian.

(The BOY taps her on the shoulder and SHE rises and follows him to the stairs.)

LITTLE GIRL: But I hope I'm not as cross as she is when I grow up. I suppose, in a way, it must be nice to be grown up. You're a big person, and they can't yell at you any more. But I won't yell. I'll be nice.

(The BOY walks down the steps and the LITTLE GIRL follows, jumping from one step to another. Just as the LITTLE GIRL reaches the last step and disappears, a man's VOICE is heard off stage.)

VOICE: Well, there you are, as solid and neat as ever. Lawn is carefully trimmed. But the ivy, it's much heavier than I remembered it—. Just like the bushes and trees along the short-cut. I'm glad you haven't changed any. I have.

SECOND GIRL: I wonder if I'll ever get used to the idea of men. It was the first time I realized that we were like animals—. Behind a bush, between wrinkled sheets, pressing against you—.

VOICE: But the stone path is a little worn, and the stones are farther apart. The fence could use a coat of paint. Well, I'll be—. It's olive drab.

(Laughs. The SOLDIER, whose voice we've heard, appears at the foot of the steps, and walks up rather fast.)

YOUNG MAN: Weren't the Greek gods human? Zeus, Hera, Aphrodite. They certainly had the frailties of human beings. But they only lived for a certain era of civilization. Ah, but they lived again in Rome. All right, two eras. Maybe I shall live for two civilizations. Good 'nuff.

SOLDIER: Well, old pickle puss is still here. Looks just the same. It might be eight years ago, and I might just be coming from school. "I guess I'll stop at the library today. Come on Irv, walk me over. I'll walk you home later." (*HE is walking about, and looking.*) I wonder if it would be hard digging a foxhole in here. (*Smiles.*) Place the gun over there. Cover—? The desk. Blow the wall off. One wall. Two walls.

LIBRARIAN: I thought he hadn't been around for a long time. Wonder what kind of a soldier he is. He never did have many pimples. Usually had that curly headed little brother with him.

SOLDIER: Aiming point! Aiming stakes—. Refer. Oh, can't you forget it? You're home now. Home. Remember? You have eight full days—ticking away. (*HE moves suddenly. Goes to catalogue.*) Always fresh flowers. The wood still has that hard, sour tang. Mmm. It smells good. Better than whiskey. Mmm. Smells so good.

FIRST GIRL: Look at the soldier boy. Not bad. No stripes—not even one. Oh, well, maybe he's just started. Soldier, how about doing my history for me?

SOLDIER: Even the books on display are the same. I wonder how many I've read here. That guy at the table looks busy. Does he realize how lucky he is being free? Being free—an individual, with your own life to live—. Freedom. Privacy. Being able to go into a bathroom, and shut the door behind you.

LIBRARIAN: Thinker, aren't you going home today? Why don't you get out and do something? Join the Army. No, don't do that. You don't belong there.

SOLDIER: This is here all the time, quiet and real. Whether I'm sweating on the gun, or drilling, or resting under a tree, it's still clean and cool here, and she's still checking out books. How I wish I could stay here forever—. Never go back. That's me at the table. I'm free, and I'm learning and thinking. That little girl coming down the steps, that's me, taking everything in. The librarian, that's me. Here for eternity.

YOUNG MAN: That soldier looks tan and healthy. It must be good to work under a hot sun, and sweat and harden and brown.

SOLDIER: What was the name of that book I wanted? (*HE goes to the LIBRARIAN at her catalogue, and speaks to her. HE smiles.*) She remembered my name. I wonder if she was surprised at my being surprised she remembered it. How in the world could she? Hundreds in here. Haven't seen her in years. Maybe she remembers the time brother upset a whole set of books.

LIBRARIAN: Remember you? Of course, I do. What do you think my life is? It's books and the people that come here to read them. My dears, I remember you all. Every one of you. Sometimes I hate you, and could choke your little throats, but soon you grow. I don't forget. You're the pulse of my life. (*SHE says something and walks to reference desk.*)

SOLDIER: She isn't so bad under that old crust of hers. A warm person. I remember the time that old deaf man came in and she had to shout to make herself heard. All the kids in the library, as if in agreement, turned and stared at her. She smiled and knew they were getting back at her. She had a sense of humor.

(The LIBRARIAN returns to desk and shakes her head. SHE offers to call another branch on the phone. The SOLDIER protests, but SHE makes the call.)

LIBRARIAN: What do you think I'm here for? I enjoy helping you. You're a nice young man. I hope you take care of yourself, when you do whatever you do.

SOLDIER: How nice she is to me. Maybe it's the uniform. No, it's not that. It's good to be remembered. She knows you and hasn't forgotten you. She'll always know you when she sees you. Maybe I've left a mark on the old neighborhood, after all. Perhaps the teachers—. I'll go over to the school and—. No. No, don't. You can't go too far back. It's no good. Disappointing—very.

YOUNG MAN: Soldier, do you think you're going to die soon? You are. I'm not. What's the difference between you and me? What's the difference between life and death?

(HE jumps up and wanders around. The LIBRARIAN gives the SOLDIER a slip. HE thanks her and walks back to the shelves.)

LIBRARIAN: Good luck, darling.

YOUNG MAN: Perhaps the answer is right in front of you and you can't see it. If I took a piece of earth and squeezed it into little grains, maybe I could squash something out.

LIBRARIAN: Are you still looking? What are you walking around for? Sit down.

YOUNG MAN: (*Goes to catalogue case and looks at flowers.*) Flowers aren't pretty. They just think they are. Perhaps they have the answer. (*HE looks closely at them, and fingers them.*)

LIBRARIAN: Crazy one, what are you doing with my flowers? You can't find anything there.

YOUNG MAN: If I could squeeze you to a pulp and get the juice and the mashed petal, I might find it. Green, sweet smelling. (*HE takes a petal between his fingers and squeezes.*)

LIBRARIAN: My flowers. (*SHE walks quietly over to the YOUNG MAN, taking his hand off the flowers, and proceeds to lecture him.*)

SOLDIER: (*During preceding business.*) Saturday morning, it was free and gay. Saturday—day of peace. The library opened early, and you'd come down the short cut, your belly full of sweet cake, and cold milk. The place was yours, yours and sour puss's.

YOUNG MAN: (*Walks away after apologizing to LIBRARIAN, and stands looking out the window.*) What's one flower? I could find out so much. How could you expect her to understand? It's late now, near dusk.

LIBRARIAN: (*Back at her desk.*) You want to destroy beauty. You're not looking for anything. That must be it.

YOUNG MAN: It's cool outside now. Why do I have to worry? I can't do everything at once. I think I'll run a few miles and eat and dance and sing and make love. (*HE turns around towards the door.*)

LIBRARIAN: (*Slightly louder.*) Are you leaving? Are you going to look and search outside? What about the book I gave you? You're not going to forget that?

YOUNG MAN: I'll feel the cold night air, and the wind. I can come back tomorrow, and start again. Tomorrow, and the day after, and the day after that. I have lots of time. All the time in the world. (*HE walks down the stairs.*)

LIBRARIAN: You've forgotten my book. You didn't want it. (*Loudly.*) Stupid, cheerful fool. What in the world are you looking for—day after day, so happy? Stupid fool, you can't answer anything. You'll never find it. You'll never find it.

(YOUNG MAN is at the steps. HE laughs out loud, exultantly, and jumps down the whole flight.)

CURTAIN

JEWEL THIEVES!

A Preposterous Comedy in Two Acts

CAST OF CHARACTERS

Gloria Desmond
Harold Busby
Alfred Blunt
Lady Lynne Fortescue

SCENE

The library in the country home of Gloria Desmond.

TIME

A day in Spring and the morning after.

ACT I

Scene 1

(The library in the country home of GLORIA DESMOND. Early afternoon. Door chimes are heard. They play the opening notes of Noel Coward's song, "I'll See You Again." No response. The chimes are heard again.)

A WOMAN'S VOICE: (*Offstage.*) Alfred?

(The chimes are heard again.)

A WOMAN'S VOICE: Alfred!? (*After a moment.*) Yes? What is it? (*After a moment.*) Yes, of course. It's right this way.

(GLORIA DESMOND, a dramatic looking woman, of "a certain age," enters followed by a solid looking MAN in his forties, with a mustache and full head of hair.)

GLORIA: There you are, my dear. You said you wanted to use the phone.

MAN: Ah, yes.

GLORIA: Well, there it is.

MAN: Lovely house.

GLORIA: Thank you.

MAN: Your face looks awfully familiar.

GLORIA: Yes, I am!

MAN: I'm a great fan of yours.

GLORIA: You must have an awfully good memory, or you're addicted to late night television.

MAN: But—you're so young.

GLORIA: "Human blood! That's what does it. A pint a day."

MAN: Don't tell me. Let me guess. "Lady Dracula." Nineteen hundred and—

GLORIA: Remarkable.

MAN: Herbert Marshall, Ian Hunter and Conrad Veidt.

GLORIA: You're a ghoul, my dear.

MAN: Is this where you live?

GLORIA: This is my country home.

MAN: Charming. Absolutely charming.

GLORIA: Would you care for a drink? A Bloody Mary, perhaps?

MAN: How kind of you.

(ALFRED BLUNT enters in the uniform of a butler; a nice looking man in his thirties.)

ALFRED: Madam, you called.

GLORIA: Alfred, my dear, what do you do in that kitchen?

ALFRED: I was polishing the silver.

GLORIA: Do you think you can spare the time to mix us a Bloody Mary?

ALFRED: Indubitably.

GLORIA: The bar's over there. You'll need some ice, some tomato juice—.

ALFRED: Worcestershire sauce, pepper, and lime. In the kitchen, no doubt.

GLORIA: You have hidden talent.

ALFRED: Thank you, madam. (*HE goes off.*)

GLORIA: He's new, but he shows great promise. You were saying—. Ah, yes. My film career.

MAN: Is it really over? Have you really retired?

GLORIA: If you were Gloria Desmond would you play mothers?

MAN: Most certainly not!

GLORIA: Besides, making pictures is very hard work. There's no time to live. To enjoy the fruit of one's labors, so to speak. You look like a business man. A robber baron. A pirate of industry.

MAN: Nothing so glamorous.

GLORIA: What do you do?

MAN: I work for the government. Is there a garage nearby, by any chance?

GLORIA: There's one in town. However, this is Sunday, you know. If you're out of gas—.

MAN: I'm afraid it's a little more serious than that. I suspect it's my carburetor. I've been stalling for the last few miles.

(ALFRED reenters with a tray containing the ingredients for the drink.)

GLORIA: Alfred—.

ALFRED: Madam?

GLORIA: I want you to call the garage. The number's in that little blue book right next to the phone.

ALFRED: Madam. (*HE sets down the tray.*) Under?

GLORIA: I beg your pardon?

ALFRED: The name of the garage.

GLORIA: It has no name. It's simply called garage.

ALFRED: Madam. (*HE proceeds to call the garage.*)

GLORIA: Have you far to go?

MAN: Not really, no.

GLORIA: You have the advantage of me.

MAN: I'm so sorry. The name is Busby.

GLORIA: Not Berkely.

MAN: Harold.

GLORIA: Busby Harold.

BUSBY: Harold Busby.

GLORIA: What do people call you? Harold sounds so—historical. I shall call you Buster. Do you mind?

ALFRED: No reply!

GLORIA: You shall spend the night. It works out perfectly. I'm one man short. I'm giving a dinner party.

BUSBY: That's very kind of you. But I do have one request. Not Buster. I had a dog named Buster. A very gentle creature. A very devoted one. Someone poisoned him.

GLORIA: Oh, how awful! Why would anyone do that?

BUSBY: He was very tenacious. Some people find that—unsettling.

GLORIA: Alfred!

ALFRED: Madam?

GLORIA: Our drinks.

ALFRED: Yes. Yes, of course. (*HE proceeds to mix the drinks.*)

GLORIA: I know nothing about you and I've invited you to be my guest. Yes. Yes, I know. Your name is Harold Busby. You work for the government. Your dog was poisoned and your carburetor is stalled.

BUSBY: I think it's defective. It's the car that stalled.

GLORIA: You're a devious man.

BUSBY: You find that offensive.

GLORIA: On the contrary. I consider it a challenge. Before you leave this house I intend to know everything about you.

BUSBY: That's a tall order.

GLORIA: I've climbed Mount Everest. Would you excuse me for a moment?

BUSBY: Certainly.

(GLORIA goes off.)

BUSBY: So you're new.

ALFRED: I beg your pardon?

BUSBY: You're new at the job.

ALFRED: This particular one.

BUSBY: You like your work?

ALFRED: It has its ups and downs. And you? Do you like yours?

BUSBY: I'm dedicated to my work.

ALFRED: Above all else?

BUSBY: Above all else.

ALFRED: It's your religion.

BUSBY: So to speak. And you? You said it has its ups and downs.

ALFRED: It's not my religion.

BUSBY: Have you a religion?

ALFRED: I'm a hedonist. I live for pleasure.

BUSBY: We all of us live for pleasure. The question is what gives us pleasure?

ALFRED: I don't wish to seem presumptuous, but aren't you being a little—presumptuous?

BUSBY: Sorry, old boy. I'm curious by nature.

ALFRED: Your drink.

BUSBY: Thank you.

ALFRED: Is it to your taste? Your drink? Is it to your taste?

BUSBY: Oh, I'll wait for your mistress to join us.

ALFRED: That may not be for quite some time. She's very busy, you see. It's Guy Fawkes Day and she's throwing this dinner party.

BUSBY: Elegant affair.

ALFRED: Oh, yes. You do have a dinner jacket, I assume.

BUSBY: Oh, yes. I often go to formal affairs.

ALFRED: As part of your job?

BUSBY: As part of my job.

ALFRED: You're not in the foreign service, are you?

BUSBY: Not as a rule.

ALFRED: But you are in the diplomatic corps.

BUSBY: Whatever gave you that idea?

ALFRED: Have you ever been to Venezuela?

BUSBY: I can't say that I have.

ALFRED: Does that mean you have or you haven't been to Venezuela?

BUSBY: Are you in the habit of giving your guests the third degree?

ALFRED: For one thing, sir, you are not my guest—.

BUSBY: And for another?

ALFRED: I'm curious by nature.

(GLORIA reenters.)

GLORIA: I'm terribly sorry. It's Guy Fawkes Day, you know—.

BUSBY: Is it?

GLORIA: Isn't it?

BUSBY: Well, I don't know.

GLORIA: At any rate I'm giving this dinner party and you're invited, of course. You do have a dinner jacket—.

BUSBY: Oh, yes.

GLORIA: I do like dressing for dinner. No one does it anymore. It gives me a chance to wear my jewels. You do like jewelry, don't you?

BUSBY: I never wear it myself.

GLORIA: Not even a ring?

BUSBY: Yes. Well, I do have this ring. That is, I did have this ring. But it disappeared.

GLORIA: Was it insured?

BUSBY: Well, no.

GLORIA: You should have had it insured. I have all my jewels insured. Not that money could ever take their place. You've heard of the Mandarin Necklace?

BUSBY: The Mandarin Necklace?

GLORIA: Surely you've heard of the Mandarin Necklace. It was given to me by my fourth, the Earl of Sedgewick shortly before his death, though his death had nothing to do with the necklace, despite all those ridiculous rumours. You shall see it tonight. It's absolutely priceless. But that's not what makes it so intriguing. It's the story that goes with it. (*SHE turns to ALFRED.*) I thought you were polishing the silver.

ALFRED: I was waiting to see if the drink was to your taste. The Bloody Mary.

GLORIA: Is the drink to your taste?

BUSBY: I was waiting for you to join me.

GLORIA: How gracious of you. To the future—whatever that may be.

BUSBY: The future.

(THEY drink.)

GLORIA: What do you think?

BUSBY: Tastes all right.

GLORIA: You've done nobly, Alfred, nobly. And now you may polish the silver.

ALFRED: Thank you, madam. (*HE goes off.*)

GLORIA: That young man has potential. Ah, yes. The Mandarin Necklace. It seems that the empress of China, Mei Ling, I believe she was called, became deathly ill. The emperor was at his wits end. The doctors had tried everything, and she was at death's door. The emperor leaned over and asked her, "Is there anything you want?" She said, "I want a beautiful necklace to wear on the journey."

BUSBY: The journey?

GLORIA: To the other world.

BUSBY: I beg your pardon. I'm not familiar with orientals.

GLORIA: So the emperor ordered his craftsmen to fashion a necklace. It was to be the most beautiful necklace in the world. And it is a stunner! Diamonds, rubies and pearls in the most delicate design. He hoped, secretly, of course, that the sight of this beautiful necklace would bring his precious wife back to life again. When she saw the beautiful necklace the eyes of the empress lit up. But unfortunately there was no improvement in her condition. She handed the dazzling necklace back to the emperor and she said, "This is too beautiful. Too beautiful. You must give this necklace to the priests as an offering to the gods."

BUSBY: Pagans were they?

GLORIA: I beg your pardon.

BUSBY: Sorry. Please go on.

GLORIA: So the emperor summoned the high priest and instructed him to display the necklace in the temple as a tribute to the gods and for all the people of China to enjoy.

BUSBY: Very democratic.

GLORIA: The high priest did as he was told. He placed the necklace on a pedestal in the temple for all the people to see and enjoy and then lo and behold there was a miracle.

BUSBY: The empress recovered. I could see that coming.

GLORIA: You have a sense of the dramatic, I see.

BUSBY: Well, actually, I did play Robin Hood once. That was in grammar school.

GLORIA: I'm sure you must have been splendid.

BUSBY: I was rather impressive, if I must say so myself, except for the fact that my tights were too tight and they split.

GLORIA: How unfortunate.

BUSBY: Played the rest of the show with my back to the wall.

GLORIA: Would you care to see my garden?

BUSBY: Nothing would please me more.

GLORIA: My begonias are a little past their prime.

BUSBY: But lovely, nevertheless, I'm sure. But you haven't finished your story.

GLORIA: Ah, yes. The Mandarin Necklace. It remained on display for centuries.

BUSBY: In the temple.

GLORIA: Until one year, one day, that is—.

BUSBY: It was stolen. Sorry.

GLORIA: There was a famine. People were starving. They begged the priests to sell the necklace, to buy food and clothing.

BUSBY: Communists, eh? I have this penchant for details. For clues.

GLORIA: The necklace wasn't stolen, for the simple fact that everyone knew that if the necklace were removed from the temple without the permission of the gods the thief would be struck dead.

BUSBY: Then how—?

GLORIA: If you will allow me! The necklace was sold. The high priest decided that human lives were far more precious than jewels. He was an idiot, of course. As everyone knows any fool can give birth to a child. Nevertheless that beautiful necklace was sold to the highest bidder, on the condition that one day the temple would be permitted to buy it back.

BUSBY: But they never have.

GLORIA: No, they never have.

BUSBY: And how, may I ask, did it come into your possession?

GLORIA: The original purchaser of the necklace was the first Earl of Sedgewick.

BUSBY: That rich, eh?

GLORIA: He bought it for his bride as a wedding gift. He died soon afterwards—of natural causes. As did all the Earls of Sedgewick. They all died young. But then the Sedgewicks have always had a penchant for death. And now, if you will follow me.

BUSBY: Yes. Yes, of course.

(GLORIA goes off to the garden. BUSBY glances about the room then follows her off. ALFRED reenters, goes to the French Doors leading to the garden and stands looking off. He's trying to remember something. HE gives up pondering, heaves a sigh, pours himself a drink and sits sipping his drink. LADY LYNNE FORTESCUE, a lovely woman in her early thirties, enters. ALFRED sets down his drink and rises.)

ALFRED: Madam.

LYNNE: You're very free with your mistress' liquor.

ALFRED: It's customary, madam, for the servants to consume their share.

LYNNE: Do you always do what's customary? I have reason to think otherwise. Where *is* your mistress?

ALFRED: In the garden, madam, with a guest.

LYNNE: Have they started to arrive already?

ALFRED: An unexpected guest—with a faulty carburetor.

LYNNE: You seem to be well informed. Is it male or female? The unexpected guest.

ALFRED: Male, ostensibly.

LYNNE: My dinner partner then. Young or old? Tall or short? Fat or thin?

ALFRED: He seems to be a man who avoids extremes of any sort.

LYNNE: Then we shall get on splendidly.

ALFRED: Those men can be dangerous. They can bore you to death. May I offer you a drink?

LYNNE: You may not.

ALFRED: May I offer you my heart?

LYNNE: If it's properly cooked.

ALFRED: Madam has a morbid sense of humor.

LYNNE: And stop calling me madam.

ALFRED: Lady Fortescue.

LYNNE: Oh, Freddy, I want to go home.

ALFRED: And so we shall.

LYNNE: Now!

ALFRED: Now, Lynnie, we've committed ourselves. I promise you. This is it. The very last time. I promise you. My word of honor.

LYNNE: You have no honor.

ALFRED: There has always been honor among thieves.

LYNNE: Daddy was right about you.

ALFRED: Your father was never right about anything. Except for once, when he took part in the creation of a most delicious creature. And even then your mother did most of the work. And your mother's mad about me.

LYNNE: My mother despises you.

ALFRED: She only thinks she does.

LYNNE: And so do I. I was perfectly respectable until I married you.

ALFRED: I have only your word for that.

LYNNE: And now I'm a thief and a fraud and a nervous wreck as well. I haven't slept a wink since I got here.

ALFRED: You only got here this morning.

LYNNE: I've been having nightmares all week. I'm sure we're going to be caught. And you didn't tell me about the curse. *He* never told us about the curse.

ALFRED: Curse? Curse? What curse?

LYNNE: You know perfectly well what curse. Whoever steals the Mandarin Necklace dies a violent death.

ALFRED: You don't really believe in all that mumbo jumbo.

LYNNE: Every Earl of Sedgewick died young.

ALFRED: But the Sedgewicks never stole the necklace.

LYNNE: The first Earl of Sedgewick was a thief. He was hung as a thief.

ALFRED: Beheaded.

LYNNE: You've known about this curse all along.

ALFRED: I refuse to acknowledge such superstitious nonsense!

(GLORIA reenters from the garden.)

GLORIA: Ah, Lady Fortescue.

LYNNE: Lynne.

GLORIA: Lynne. I'm so glad you could make it.

LYNNE: Eric asked me to give you his apologies. It's his leg, you know.

GLORIA: The wooden one?

LYNNE: No, the other one. Gout.

GLORIA: He drinks too much. Has my butler been amusing you?

LYNNE: Not really, no.

GLORIA: I hope he hasn't forgotten his place. (*To ALFRED.*) Have you been behaving yourself?

ALFRED: Really, madam!

LYNNE: I didn't mean to imply—.

GLORIA: That's quite all right. He's an impertinent fellow and I knew straight off that I should have to take him in hand.

LYNNE: Servants can be a bother.

ALFRED: If my services are no longer required—.

GLORIA: I never said that. But you may go—for the nonce.

ALFRED: Madam has but to ring.

GLORIA: The doorbell rang three times.

ALFRED: Was that the doorbell? I thought they were sound effects. (*HE goes off.*)

GLORIA: He shall be replaced. That's quite all right. He was only a stopgap, an emergency measure to fill a temporary vacancy. My regular butler was suddenly called away. Illness in the family, I believe.

Or was it a funeral? They come so thick and fast—. But you know nothing about such things, my dear. You're so pretty—for a Fortescue.

LYNNE: I'm not really. What I mean to say—.

GLORIA: Yes. Yes, of course. Dear Donald.

LYNNE: Roger.

GLORIA: Roger? I thought Roger was still alive.

LYNNE: So he is. We've been divorced for quite some time.

GLORIA: Ah, yes. But that's a little like death, my dear. Is it not? And I should know. I divorced my second, my third and my fifth. So you're a friend of Eric's, my dear.

LYNNE: An acquaintance, really. We met in Monte Carlo.

GLORIA: He spoke so warmly of you. I gather he's quite smitten. Which is rather unusual for Eric. Oh, not that he doesn't have a weakness for a pretty face. But Eric's so—so.

LYNNE: Teutonic!

GLORIA: Exactly. He's not a baron, you know.

LYNNE: Oh?

GLORIA: Not officially, that is, He got his start in life as a dance instructor, ballroom, that is. I hope that doesn't offend your British sensibility. You are British, aren't you?

LYNNE: I used to be. But the British have become so grubby. They're not even shopkeepers any longer.

GLORIA: There is no elegance in the world anymore. Even cleanliness. In Amsterdam, where the housewives used to scour their sidewalks every morning, one has to be careful where one steps. Apropos, we have a dinner partner for you.

LYNNE: Oh?

GLORIA: An unexpected guest. He claims to work for the government. You must excuse me. Your dinner partner, incidentally, is in the garden. He's been admiring my begonias. He claims to be Harold Busby.

LYNNE: Harold Busby?

GLORIA: Is he an acquaintance of yours?

LYNNE: I did know a Busby Harold, and he was rather backward.

GLORIA: Truth is stranger than fiction.

(SHE goes off. LYNNE stands thinking for a moment, then goes to the French doors leading to the garden. As SHE stands looking toward the garden BUSBY enters from the opposite door.)

BUSBY: Lady Fortescue?

LYNNE: (*SHE whirls about.*) Who are you?

BUSBY: Busby at your service.

LYNNE: Harold?

BUSBY: Why, yes.

LYNNE: Busby Harold?

BUSBY: Well, actually it's Harold Busby.

LYNNE: Are you quite certain?

BUSBY: The one certainty in life is that nothing is certain.

LYNNE: You're a philosopher.

BUSBY: I have never claimed to be a philosopher, though I have been known to be philosophical from time to time. I'm in government.

LYNNE: May I ask to which branch of the government you're attached?

BUSBY: You may.

LYNNE: I suspect you're inclined to be mysterious.

BUSBY: Society being what it is, what choice does one have? I understand I'm to be your partner at dinner.

LYNNE: You'll be replacing Eric Von Steuben.

BUSBY: Baron Von Steuben?

LYNNE: Ostensibly. I came as his guest.

BUSBY: He's been detained—.

LYNNE: Unavoidably.

BUSBY: The game's afoot then is it not?

LYNNE: I beg your pardon.

BUSBY: The treasure hunt. Have you seen it?

LYNNE: It?

BUSBY: The Mandarin Necklace? Come, come, come. We both know why we're here. You don't trust me and, of course, there's no reason why you should. Suppose I were to tell you that Harry the Snake and I—.

LYNNE: I'm afraid you must have me confused with someone else.

BUSBY: The Farnum Affair!

LYNNE: Felix?

BUSBY: Felicia! The Carter Case!

LYNNE: Cigarette?

BUSBY: You've been to the Riviera, have you not?

LYNNE: French or Italian?

BUSBY: The coast of Madagascar!

(ALFRED enters.)

ALFRED: May I be of service?

BUSBY: Do you know where it is? Do you know where she keeps it?

ALFRED: Specifically?

BUSBY: Exactly.

LYNNE: I'm afraid Mr. Harold—.

BUSBY: Busby.

ALFRED: Busby Harold?

LYNNE & BUSBY: Harold Busby.

LYNNE: Is a bit confused.

BUSBY: Willy the Weasel.

ALFRED: Louie the louse.

BUSBY: Louie the louse?

ALFRED: Winnie the pooh?

LYNNE: Spot the dog.

ALFRED: Dumbo the elephant.

LYNNE: Bambi the deer.

ALFRED: Mickey the mouse.

BUSBY: I'm sorry. I thought we might be friends. It's every man for himself then, is it not? (*HE goes off.*)

LYNNE: Who is he?

ALFRED: He's not Harold Busby.

LYNNE: Nor is he Busby Harold.

ALFRED: Does he work for the government, do you think?

LYNNE: He seems to know Eric. He knows of him, at any rate.

ALFRED: I don't trust him.

LYNNE: And I don't trust Eric.

ALFRED: Just because he wears a monocle. Eric, that is.

LYNNE: It's not the monocle. It's his eyes. They're false. And if he knows Eric—.

ALFRED: Surely you don't think that—.

LYNNE: I don't see why not. We're in deep waters, my dear, and there are sharks about.

GLORIA: (*Offstage.*) Alfred?

LYNNE: And a barracuda.

(GLORIA enters.)

GLORIA: It's time for tea. I thought we might have our tea in the garden. (*To ALFRED.*) Have you ever poured?

ALFRED: Time and time again.

GLORIA: If you have no further use for Alfred—.

LYNNE: We were discussing horses.

GLORIA: Do you ride?

LYNNE: No, I play.

GLORIA: You're a gambler.

LYNNE: Only when the odds are in my favor.

GLORIA: There's no fun in playing it safe, my dear. Come along, Arthur—.

ALFRED: Alfred.

GLORIA: You'll join us, won't you, Lady Fortescue.

(SHE goes off, followed by ALFRED.)

LYNNE: Now, why did she call him Arthur? (*SHE goes off.*)

END OF ACT I, SCENE 1

ACT I

Scene 2

(BUSBY, in dinner jacket, enters, looks about and picks up the phone. HE dials, waits a moment, cuts himself off, dials again, cuts himself off then dials a third time.)

BUSBY: The rain in Spain. The Spaniards are noted for their begonias, except in the south where the pom poms grow—in profusion. Guy Fawkes Day—in Venezuela. Louie the louse. Dumbo, Bambi and Mickey Mouse.

(ALFRED enters with a duster, and proceeds to dust.)

BUSBY: I'm afraid you have the wrong number. (*HE hangs up.*) Did you overhear what I said?

ALFRED: To the wrong number?

BUSBY: Yes. Well, it does get lonely at times.

ALFRED: You're not married.

BUSBY: Have you thought over my proposition?

ALFRED: I am. Married, that is.

BUSBY: What has that got to do with it?

ALFRED: Which proposition were you referring to?

BUSBY: Will you stop that infernal dusting?

ALFRED: Why are you here?

BUSBY: I'm here for the same reason you are.

ALFRED: Then there's nothing wrong with your carburetor.

BUSBY: It's missing.

ALFRED: How can you possibly drive without a carburetor?

BUSBY: Exactly.

ALFRED: But that's insane. It's easy enough to trace a missing carburetor.

BUSBY: Oh, it'll turn up at the proper time. Look, there's no reason why we can't be friends.

ALFRED: Do you make it a habit of befriending butlers?

BUSBY: You're not a butler and you know it.

ALFRED: And what makes you so sure of that?

BUSBY: Because butlers never dust. That's the maid's job. I've worked as a butler, you see. The Carter case.

ALFRED: Oh, not again!

(A gong is heard.)

BUSBY: What on earth was that?

ALFRED: The dinner bell.

BUSBY: But there's no one here, except for Lady Fortescue—so called, and myself.

(Oriental music is heard.)

ALFRED: Madam's a great one for sound effects.

(LYNNE enters, beautifully gowned.)

ALFRED: Did you strike that gong?

LYNNE: I couldn't resist.

ALFRED: That gown is rather low cut.

LYNNE: Don't be such a prude.

ALFRED: (*To BUSBY.*) What are you staring at?

BUSBY: When something's on display, one looks at it.

ALFRED: Yes. Well, just make sure that's all you do.

LYNNE: Oh, really, Freddy!

BUSBY: Freddy, is it? Freddy the Fox?

LYNNE: Freddy the fool.

BUSBY: You two are a team.

ALFRED & LYNNE: A team? That's ridiculous!

BUSBY: Have it your way. (*HE goes off.*)

ALFRED: Well?

LYNNE: No luck.

ALFRED: You went too late.

LYNNE: Too soon apparently. It was nowhere in sight. There was a jewel box.

ALFRED: Aha!

LYNNE: It wasn't there.

ALFRED: How do you know?

LYNNE: Because I had her open it. These earrings are hers. Don't upset yourself. They're paste, though she pretends they're not.

ALFRED: What's the world coming to? It gives one pause.

LYNNE: Oh, Freddy—.

ALFRED: Lynnie, please! We've come this far. You look awfully sexy in that dress. Stern, but sexy.

LYNNE: Oh, Freddy. (*HE takes her in his arms, bends her over and kisses her.*)

(The Gong is heard.)

ALFRED: What are we thinking of?

(HE releases her and continues dusting. The oriental music is heard and BUSBY enters.)

LYNNE: Did you strike that gong?

BUSBY: And what if I did?

ALFRED: It's not a toy, you know.

BUSBY: It's eight o'clock. Where are the guests? Where's Miss Desmond?

LYNNE: She's getting dressed.

ALFRED: I'm absolutely starved.

(The gong is heard.)

LYNNE: Oh, really!

BUSBY: That must be her.

(The oriental music is heard and GLORIA enters wearing a striking oriental gown—and a black wig.)

GLORIA: Very effective, don't you think? The gong, that is. It belonged to the emperor ChooChoo Foo. It was struck every time a head was struck off.

BUSBY: That's ghoulish. Look, I don't wish to seem rude, but it is eight o'clock, and I'm absolutely starved.

GLORIA: If you're hungry there are things to nibble on on the terrace. Alfred, did you light the lanterns?

ALFRED: Indubitably.

BUSBY: I say! You're not wearing the necklace.

GLORIA: How observant of you! Alfred, what on earth are you doing?

ALFRED: Dusting, madam.

GLORIA: Well, you needn't be so intense about it. You'll wear yourself out, and we wouldn't want that. Now would we?

LYNNE: I'm terribly disappointed. I've heard so much about that fabulous necklace. I was so looking forward to it.

GLORIA: Well, I haven't quite decided yet—whether to wear it or not.

LYNNE: But you were planning to, were you not?

GLORIA: Oh, yes.

LYNNE: May I ask what changed your mind?

GLORIA: I've been speaking to my astrologer.

LYNNE: And what did he say?

GLORIA: It's a she.

LYNNE: What did she say?

GLORIA: The moon is on the cusp.

LYNNE: What does that mean?

GLORIA: It means that things are unsettled. It means that it's quite possible that Venus might collide with Mars.

BUSBY: That's ridiculous!

GLORIA: Are you an astrologer?

BUSBY: I'm an amateur astronomer.

GLORIA: Then you're not a professional.

BUSBY: I may not be a professional but I know my stars.

GLORIA: Venus is a planet and so is Mars and its orbit, Mars, that is, is very eccentric.

BUSBY: So are the stars.

GLORIA: Be that as it may, and that may very well be, but I've been told—and in no uncertain terms—that there's danger in the air.

LYNNE: What sort of danger?

GLORIA: She didn't say.

BUSBY: I thought you said—.

GLORIA: I most certainly did not.

BUSBY: You most certainly did.

LYNNE: Oh, really! I'm sorry. It's that infernal gong. It's terribly unnerving.

BUSBY: And now, if you'll excuse me, I'm going to nibble on something. (*HE goes off.*)

GLORIA: That's a very annoying man. I'm sorry I invited him. But what could I do? Alfred!

ALFRED: Madam!

GLORIA: Stop dusting and pour me a drink.

ALFRED: The usual?

GLORIA: I like to be surprised. Would you care for a drink, my dear?

LYNNE: Not right now, thank you.

GLORIA: Have you any children, my dear?

LYNNE: No. Not yet.

GLORIA: I have three. All illegitimate. I refused to have an abortion, fashionable as they were at the time. Each time I went into the hills with my faithful Indian maid.

LYNNE: Where are they now?

GLORIA: Scattered, my dear. Scattered about the world. The boy's an anthropologist. He digs in foreign soil. The girl's an aviatrix. She's up there somewhere.

LYNNE: And the third?

GLORIA: Gone. Disappeared. Vanished from the face of the earth. Apparently my Indian maid was not as faithful as all that. She absconded with my third. It was a difficult birth. I almost died. I was feverish, delirious and I must have passed out immediately after delivery. When I awoke I was all alone in this cabin, at the top of the mountain, surrounded by wind and snow. I was too weak to move and my child, my little baby, was nowhere to be seen.

LYNNE: Was it a boy or a girl?

GLORIA: One assumes it was one or the other.

ALFRED: Not necessarily.

LYNNE: How awful for you! But I don't understand. Weren't you married at the time?

GLORIA: My timing on the screen has always been impeccable. Unfortunately life is not that manageable. I searched the world over, but there was no trace of the maid—or the child.

LYNNE: Perhaps she returned to India.

GLORIA: She was an American Indian. I have always been patriotic, and that's the thanks I got.

LYNNE: I'm sorry, I—.

GLORIA: That's quite all right, my dear. Life isn't all sunshine and roses. That's why I think it's so important to surround oneself with beauty. And you must do the same, my dear. How long has it been since you lost Lord Fortescue.

LYNNE: Why—.

ALFRED: Your drink, madam.

GLORIA: Thank you, dear. You must envelope yourself with love. Failing that—lots and lots of money.

LYNNE: Don't you think that money's a poor substitute?

GLORIA: Don't use that word.

LYNNE: Substitute?

GLORIA: Poor! It's an ugly word. It's obscene. I've traveled the world over and I've seen poverty. And there was a time—. Well, we won't go into that. But I resolved long ago that I would never be poor. Physically or spiritually.

LYNNE: May I ask who your astrologer is?

GLORIA: Estralita. That's the name she goes by, at any rate. Why do you ask?

LYNNE: Nothing, really.

GLORIA: You must have had a reason.

LYNNE: I'm something of a psychic myself.

GLORIA: Are you really? Metaphysical?

LYNNE: Let's just say that I deal in auras. Your butler, for example, has a most interesting aura. When were you born, my good man? No, don't tell me. You're a Libra, are you not?

ALFRED: You're the psychic.

GLORIA: Come, come, Alfred. Don't be a spoilsport.

LYNNE: That's quite all right. His type is quite common.

GLORIA: How interesting. Do you read palms?

LYNNE: I don't make a habit of it.

GLORIA: What can you tell me about Alfred?

LYNNE: Alfred, I would say, has a bit of the snake about him.

ALFRED: You mean I'm a charmer.

GLORIA: Don't interrupt. Do go on.

LYNNE: As a boy he collected butterflies—and pinned them to the wall.

ALFRED: A specimen sheet.

LYNNE: At his parents' request he ran away from home—and joined the circus—as a clown.

GLORIA: Is all this true?

ALFRED: Well, yes, but I was adopted.

GLORIA: Were you an orphan?

ALFRED: Well, yes. I spent my early childhood in an orphanage.

GLORIA: Where?

ALFRED: In the south of China. It may have been the north. I don't recall. I was very young at the time.

GLORIA: How did you get there?

ALFRED: No one seems to know.

GLORIA: You're not Chinese.

ALFRED: Not that I know of. However, I've always had a facility for languages.

LYNNE: Your left leg is shorter than your right?

ALFRED: It's never been a handicap.

LYNNE: And your eyes are blue.

ALFRED: One of them.

GLORIA: But this is amazing. Tell me, my dear, can you read everyone's aura? Can you read mine? Why do you turn away like that? What do you see?

LYNNE: Nothing.

GLORIA: You're not telling me the truth.

LYNNE: Some things are better left unsaid.

GLORIA: You're frightening me.

(The telephone rings. ALFRED answers it.)

ALFRED: Miss Desmond's residence. There's no one here by that name. You're not referring to a Mr. Harold Busby, by any chance? Hello? Hello? (*HE hangs up.*) The wrong number.

GLORIA: I insist that you read my aura. You saw something. What did you see?

LYNNE: I saw—.

GLORIA: Yes, yes. Go on.

LYNNE: It was very faint. I saw this woman—. On her death bed, it would seem. She looked Chinese.

GLORIA: Mei Ling. The Empress of China.

LYNNE: She kept touching her throat—as if she were feeling for something that was missing.

GLORIA: The necklace. The Mandarin Necklace. She would have wanted me to wear it, I know. The fact of the matter is—. Well, it's that awful man. I don't trust him. He's not what he seems to be.

LYNNE: What do you think he really is?

GLORIA: He's a thief. I'm sure of it.

LYNNE: And what makes you think that?

ALFRED: Well, he does have shifty eyes.

GLORIA: It's not his eyes so much. It's that mustache. It droops. It sags—very suspiciously. Have you noticed?

ALFRED: And his hair and his mustache are different colors.

GLORIA: Exactly! It's foolish, I know. The fact of the matter is this party's just an excuse to show off my necklace. I don't even know when Guy Fawkes Day takes place.

ALFRED: November fifth, sixteen oh five. It's my birthday. The day of the month, that is. Not the year.

LYNNE: But what's the joy of owning something beautiful if you can't even enjoy it? If you can't share it with your friends.

GLORIA: You're quite right, of course. As long as I'm not left alone with him.

LYNNE & ALFRED: We'll see to that.

ALFRED: The guests should be arriving any moment now.

GLORIA: I'll do it. I'll wear the necklace!

LYNNE: Would you like me to come upstairs with you?

GLORIA: What I would like you to do is to keep that Busby man occupied. He's probably on the terrace stuffing that false face of his.

LYNNE: Why, yes. Yes, of course. Unless, of course—.

GLORIA: Thank you, dear.

LYNNE: Yes. Yes, of course. (*SHE hesitates and goes off to the interior of the house.*)

ALFRED: I won't leave your side.

GLORIA: You're very loyal, my dear. Loyal and true.

ALFRED: Madam.

GLORIA: And I know that I can count on you in a pinch. But for now—.

ALFRED: Yes?

GLORIA: I'd like you to go into the conservatory and tell the trio that they can start to play.

ALFRED: Now?

GLORIA: Yes, now.

ALFRED: Your wish is my command. (*HE starts off very slowly.*)

GLORIA: And Alfred—.

ALFRED: (*HE stops immediately.*) Madam?

GLORIA: When the guests arrive you can direct them to the terrace.

ALFRED: Madam. (*HE starts off again.*)

GLORIA: Oh, and Alfred—.

ALFRED: Madam?

GLORIA: You must announce their names loudly and clearly—and you mustn't be alarmed.

ALFRED: Alarmed?

GLORIA: When you hear their names.

ALFRED: I see. Is there anything else?

GLORIA: That will do, my dear, for now.

(HE starts off and stops.)

GLORIA: Yes? What is it?

ALFRED: Nothing, Madam. (*HE starts off.*)

GLORIA: Oh, and Alfred.

(HE stops.)

GLORIA: The duster.

ALFRED: Thank you, madam.

(ALFRED goes off with the duster. GLORIA sighs apprehensively. SHE goes to the French doors and looks out into the garden, then goes to the other door and looks out. The trio is heard playing very softly offstage. GLORIA goes to one of the paintings on the wall and swings it aside—it's on hinges. SHE proceeds to dial open the safe concealed behind the picture. SHE removes from the safe a velvet covered jewel case, opens the case and takes from it the dazzling Mandarin Necklace. SHE admires it, kisses it then puts it around her neck, returns the box to the safe, closes the safe and replaces the picture. SHE stands in front of the mirror, admiring the necklace on her person then suddenly whirls about to face BUSBY, standing in the open French doors. The TWO stand staring at each other. The door chimes are heard loudly and clearly. "I'll See You Again." After a moment ALFRED is heard.)

ALFRED: (*Offstage.*) Miss Mary Pickford and Mr. Charles Chaplin.

BUSBY: It's more beautiful than I'd ever imagined.

(Door chimes. "I'll See You Again.")

ALFRED: (*Offstage.*) Miss Joan Crawford and Mr. Clark Gable. Miss Jean Harlow and Mr. Humphrey Bogart.

(BUSBY approaches GLORIA. SHE shrinks back. HE extends his arm.)

BUSBY: May I?

(GLORIA apprehensively places her hand on his arm.)

ALFRED: (*Offstage.*) Miss Theda Bara and Mr. Rudolph Valentino.

(Chimes. "I'll See You Again.")

ALFRED: (*Offstage.*) Miss Norma Shearer and Mr. John Barrymore.

(GLORIA and BUSBY go slowly off to the interior of the house.)

END OF ACT 1, SCENE 2

ACT II

Scene 1

(Four hours later. LYNNE enters in her evening gown and sits with a sigh. ALFRED enters a moment later.)

LYNNE: Did you get a look at Rudolph Valentino? He came up to here on me. (*Indicating her bosom.*) And I could have sworn he had make-up on.

ALFRED: Just a little rouge.

LYNNE: And lots of mascara.

ALFRED: And what about Mary Pickford? At least two hundred pounds.

LYNNE: Where did she find all those creatures?

ALFRED: In the social register.

LYNNE: Where's the safe?

ALFRED: I don't know. It must be in this room. Busby must know. He was in here when she took the necklace out of the safe.

LYNNE: Maybe we ought to cut him in.

ALFRED: Not unless we absolutely have to.

(BUSBY enters.)

BUSBY: So, here we are. Interesting array of guests, were they not? I've never seen a gown like that. I mean the one on Theda Bara. Most of the back was missing.

LYNNE: We—I mean I was wondering where you disappeared to, just before the guests arrived.

BUSBY: Disappeared?

LYNNE: You said you were going to the terrace to get something to nibble on.

BUSBY: And so I did.

LYNNE: You weren't there very long.

ALFRED: You were in here when Miss Desmond took the necklace out of the safe.

BUSBY: Was I?

ALFRED: I saw you come out of here with her. She wasn't wearing the necklace when she came into this room. She was wearing it when she came out.

BUSBY: For a man with one blue eye you're very observant.

ALFRED: I wouldn't try anything funny, if I were you.

BUSBY: I'm not the comic type.

ALFRED: Dedicated you said. Your work is your religion.

BUSBY: Did I say that? I have always admired the inscrutable. There was an English film actor named George Sanders. He was my favorite. Nothing ever moved when he spoke.

ALFRED: That's a physical impossibility.

BUSBY: Nothing is impossible. They've put a man on the moon, have they not?

ALFRED: There's a rumor going about that that was all a hoax.

BUSBY: Impossible! I mean—.

ALFRED: Yes? What do you mean?

BUSBY: I'm not accustomed to being subjected to the third degree.

LYNNE: We think otherwise.

BUSBY: We?

LYNNE: I was using the royal we. The editorial we. I am a widow, you know.

BUSBY: Have you the death certificate to prove it?

LYNNE: (*She reaches into her bosom, pulls out a document and hands it to BUSBY.*) I think you'll find that all in order.

BUSBY: (*Examines the document and hands it back to LYNNE.*) And how do I know this isn't a forgery?

ALFRED: How dare you malign the dead?

BUSBY: Alfred is it? Alfred what?

ALFRED: Alfred Blunt.

BUSBY: A likely story.

ALFRED: It's as good a name as Busby, Harold.

BUSBY: It's Harold Busby.

ALFRED: What about "wrong number"?

BUSBY: What about it?

LYNNE: And missing carburetor?

BUSBY: Who told you my carburetor was missing?

ALFRED: Isn't it?

BUSBY: Most certainly not. It's in my possession.

LYNNE: I thought as much.

ALFRED: And you do answer to the wrong number—.

BUSBY: Only when I'm addressed as such.

ALFRED: At any rate a call came for you—or maybe it wasn't for you—while you were supposedly out on the terrace. They asked specifically for "the wrong number."

BUSBY: Who was it from?

ALFRED: They didn't say.

BUSBY: Didn't you ask?

ALFRED: Well, of course, I asked.

BUSBY: And?

ALFRED: They hung up.

BUSBY: You should have taken the message. That's part of the butler's job, to take messages. What sort of a butler are you?

LYNNE: Why are you so upset?

BUSBY: What on earth makes you think that I'm upset.

ALFRED: The way you keep clenching and unclenching your fists.

BUSBY: That's merely an exercise—to strengthen my grip. It just so happens that I play tennis. I've played tennis all my life. Since I was old enough to hold a racket.

ALFRED: And how old were you then?

BUSBY: I don't recall exactly.

LYNNE: I thought as much.

ALFRED: And you can't deny that your code name—.

BUSBY: Code name?

LYNNE: Alias.

ALFRED: Pseudonym.

LYNNE & ALFRED: Is wrong number.

BUSBY: Wrong number, indeed! Why that might apply to anyone—anyone at that dinner table this evening. You're barking up the wrong tree, my friends.

LYNNE: Barking?

ALFRED: Tree?

BUSBY: That's a simile.

LYNNE: Sounds more like a metaphor to me.

ALFRED: I never could get them straight.

BUSBY: Yes!

ALFRED: What was that supposed to mean?

BUSBY: If the shoe fits.

LYNNE: That was definitely a metaphor.

BUSBY: The old changing the subject routine, eh?

(GLORIA enters.)

GLORIA: I thought they'd never leave. I'm absolutely exhausted.

ALFRED: A drink, madam?

GLORIA: And why not? Did you enjoy yourself, my dear?

LYNNE: It was a most interesting evening. But there's one thing I don't understand.

GLORIA: Only one. How very perceptive of you. The important thing is, however, were you bored?

LYNNE: Not really, no.

GLORIA: Then that's all that really matters, my dear. Boredom is the greatest killer of all. The most deadly of diseases and it knows no class, no sex, no nationality. It's a disease that's universal.

LYNNE: Were all those jewels really genuine?

GLORIA: What do you think, my dear?

LYNNE: Well, I'm not an expert—.

BUSBY: Ha!

GLORIA: Mr. Busby? You were going to say?

ALFRED: Your drink, madam!

GLORIA: Thank you, my dear. You did nobly, by the way.

ALFRED: Thank you, madam. One does one's best.

GLORIA: I think they were properly impressed, were they not?

LYNNE: And they had every reason to be. The food and the service were both excellent.

GLORIA: Trivialities, my dear. Trivialities. I'm referring to my treasure. My baby. The light of my life. My Mandarin Necklace.

ALFRED: It put all the others to shame.

LYNNE: It really is a marvel, Miss Desmond.

GLORIA: Gloria. Would you like to try it on?

LYNNE: May I?

(BUSBY clears his throat.)

GLORIA: Mr. Busby?

ALFRED: May I be of any assistance?

GLORIA: Yes, of course. Why don't you do the honors.

ALFRED: I should be honored.

(HE removes the necklace from GLORIA and places it on LYNNE.)

GLORIA: Gently, my dear. Gently. Mr. Busby, is there anything wrong?

BUSBY: Wrong?

GLORIA: You look so—apprehensive.

BUSBY: Apprehensive? Nonsense! What is there to be apprehensive about?

GLORIA: Then why do you keep clenching and unclenching your fists like that?

BUSBY: It's a nervous habit of mine.

ALFRED: I thought, sir, it was an exercise to strengthen your fingers.

BUSBY: So it is. It happens to be both. I kill two birds with one stone, so to speak.

GLORIA: How cruel of you.

BUSBY: It was merely—.

ALFRED: A metaphor.

BUSBY: Yes, a metaphor.

GLORIA: You should wear more jewelry, my dear. It's expensive, I know, but it's worth it.

LYNNE: It's priceless! Absolutely priceless!

BUSBY: Everything has its price, Lady Fortescue, does it not? Lady Fortescue?

LYNNE: I beg your pardon. I mustn't hold onto this too long, or I should never want to give it back.

BUSBY: That would be theft.

GLORIA: Really, Mr. Busby!

BUSBY: I believe in calling—.

ALFRED: A spade a spade?

BUSBY: The cards as I see them.

GLORIA: You play cards, Mrs. Busby.

BUSBY: I've dealt a few decks in my time.

ALFRED: There's no end to your talents, sir.

BUSBY: Everyone has talent. Few people take the trouble to exercise their gifts.

LYNNE: It's so stuffy in here.

GLORIA: Perhaps you'd like to take a turn in the garden.

LYNNE: It is a lovely night.

BUSBY: That's an excellent idea. May I join you, Lady Fortescue? We wouldn't want that precious necklace to walk about unprotected, would we?

GLORIA: How solicitous of you, Mr. Busby!

BUSBY: It's my nature, Miss Desmond. Since childhood I have always deplored injustice. Law and order! That's my motto.

ALFRED: Honesty is the best policy.

LYNNE: He who steals my purse steals trash.

GLORIA: The night has a thousand eyes.

BUSBY: Nineteen forty eight. Edward G. Robinson. Gail Russel. John Lund and Virginia Bruce. Paramount Pictures. Directed by John Farrow, I believe.

GLORIA: You amaze me, Mr. Busby.

BUSBY: I have total recall.

ALFRED: That must be a terrible burden.

BUSBY: One learns to live with it.

GLORIA: That's the danger, my dear. Is it not?

LYNNE: I'm terribly tired. I think I'll turn in. Yes. Yes, of course, the necklace. What am I thinking of?

ALFRED: Allow me, Lady Fortescue.

LYNNE: Thank you, Alfred.

ALFRED: Ne pas de quoi.

BUSBY: You speak Italian, I see.

ALFRED: That was French.

(HE removes the necklace from LYNNE and places it on GLORIA.)

ALFRED: Madam.

GLORIA: Thank you, my dear.

ALFRED: That clasp is loose. It really should be replaced.

BUSBY: May I? (*HE takes a jeweler's magnifying glass from his pocket and examines the clasp.*) Most interesting. That clasp is new, is it not?

GLORIA: Why, yes.

BUSBY: I thought as much. One can't be too careful.

GLORIA: It's been my experience that one can.

LYNNE: And now if you'll excuse me.

GLORIA: Yes, course, my dear. Pleasant dreams.

LYNNE: Thank you. Good night, Mr. Busby.

BUSBY: Good night. Lady Fortescue.

(LYNNE turns on her heels and goes off.)

GLORIA: Charming girl. Absolutely charming.

BUSBY: Do you know her well?

GLORIA: Does anyone know anyone—really well? Alfred, by the way, has been able to get in touch with Mr. Townsend.

BUSBY: Mr. Townsend?

GLORIA: The owner of the garage. The mechanic will be here first thing in the morning.

BUSBY: What time would that be?

GLORIA: Alfred?

ALFRED: Madam?

GLORIA: What time are we expecting Mr. Townsend's mechanic?

ALFRED: First thing in the morning.

BUSBY: What time would that be?

ALFRED: Very bright and very early—I should imagine.

BUSBY: Bright and early is relative.

ALFRED: Relative to what?

BUSBY: To one's individual habits.

ALFRED: I'm happy to say I know nothing of Mr. Townsend's individual habits.

GLORIA: If you're to get a good night's sleep, Mr. Busby—.

BUSBY: Yes. Yes, of course. Incidentally, I'm a very light sleeper—in case you should happen to need any assistance.

GLORIA: Why on earth should I need any assistance? I happen to be in excellent health, Mr. Busby, and if I should happen to need any assistance, there's Alfred here.

ALFRED: Indubitably.

BUSBY: It's been my experience—.

ALFRED: I'm not sure that Miss Desmond's particularly interested in your experience. Are we, Miss Desmond?

GLORIA: Well, now that all depends. Has your experience been unique, Mr. Busby?

BUSBY: Each one of us is unique.

GLORIA: I don't think so, Mr. Busby. Pleasant dreams.

(BUSBY clicks his heels, nods and goes off.)

GLORIA: He makes me very uneasy.

ALFRED: His table manners left much to be desired.

GLORIA: What did you think of my friends, my dear.

ALFRED: I never judge a book by its cover.

GLORIA: That's where we differ, my dear. Appearance is all. I'm terribly tense.

ALFRED: Would madam like me to massage her neck?

GLORIA: Is that something that you do well?

ALFRED: Notoriously.

GLORIA: Let me see your fingers. Ah, yes.

ALFRED: Shall I remove the necklace?

GLORIA: Is that absolutely necessary?

ALFRED: It would make things easier.

GLORIA: Let's leave the necklace where it is.

(ALFRED massages her neck.)

GLORIA: Mmmmm. Magical fingers. Naughty fingers. Thank you, my dear.

ALFRED: Would madam like me to return the necklace to its proper place?

GLORIA: I think I can manage that by myself. You might stand guard. In case that awful Mr. Busby should come snooping about.

ALFRED: Where would madam like me to stand?

GLORIA: Just outside the door.

ALFRED: Yes. Yes, of course. (*HE stands in the doorway.*)

GLORIA: Outside that door, my dear.

ALFRED: Yes. Yes, of course. (*HE goes off.*)

(GLORIA goes quickly to the French doors and locks them. SHE then returns the necklace to the safe and replaces the picture.)

GLORIA: Alfred?

ALFRED: (*Offstage.*) Madam?

GLORIA: You may reenter now.

(ALFRED reenters.)

GLORIA: All seems to be in order now, does it not?

ALFRED: One hopes so, madam.

GLORIA: Then you may kiss me good night.

ALFRED: Madam?

GLORIA: You are just a stopgap, my dear.

ALFRED: Yes. Yes, of course.

(GLORIA extends her cheek and HE kisses it.)

GLORIA: You don't walk in your sleep, I trust.

ALFRED: Not for quite some time.

GLORIA: My door shall be firmly shut.

(SHE goes off. ALFRED looks about the room. GLORIA reenters.)

GLORIA: You will make sure all the lights are out.

ALFRED: Madam.

(SHE goes off. ALFRED walks about the room, examining it.)

GLORIA: (*Offstage.*) Alfred? The lights!

ALFRED: Madam.

(HE shuts the lights and goes off. Darkness. Silence. Someone tries to open the French doors and finally gives up on them. Silence. A clock strikes two. Silence. A figure enters from the other door. A flashlight is shone about the room. Drawers are opened. Pictures are examined. The picture that conceals the safe is approached. The flashlight is suddenly turned off. A second person enters the room. A flashlight is shone about. Drawers are opened. Pictures are examined. The picture concealing the safe is approached. The flashlight's turned off. It's turned on again and comes to rest on LYNNE, in a dressing gown, cowering in the corner.)

LYNNE: I—ah—couldn't sleep.

ALFRED: You were supposed to wait for me.

LYNNE: Oh, it's you. You took so long.

ALFRED: Have you found it?

LYNNE: No. Not yet. It's got to be behind that picture over there.

(SHE shines her flashlight on the picture and ALFRED tries to move it, with no luck.)

LYNNE: What's the matter?

ALFRED: It doesn't move. It must be nailed to the wall.

LYNNE: Maybe it's on a hinge.

ALFRED: (*HE swings the picture away from the wall.*) What would I do without you?

LYNNE: What does it look like? Hard or easy.

ALFRED: It's hard to say. Maybe you'd better stand guard.

LYNNE: Yes, master. (*SHE turns off her flashlight and stands guard at the door.*)

ALFRED: Damn!

LYNNE: How's it coming? Freddy?

ALFRED: Oh, do shut up!

LYNNE: Sorry.

ALFRED: I shall have to start all over again.

LYNNE: Do hurry, dear! What's that noise?

ALFRED: Voila! (*HE turns the flashlight on the open safe, removes the case, then the necklace holding it up to admire it.*) That really is a beauty!

LYNNE: It's certainly worth more than forty thousand dollars.

ALFRED: Let's not be greedy. After all, if it weren't for Eric neither of us would be here.

LYNNE: Do hurry, dear.

ALFRED: (*HE slips the necklace into his left pocket and produces the duplicate from his right.*) Now who could tell the difference? (*ALFRED places the duplicate in the case. The clock chimes the quarter hour.*)

LYNNE: Oh, good Lord!

ALFRED: What's the matter? Did you hear anything?

LYNNE: Not really, no! It's that damn clock!

(ALFRED replaces the case and closes the safe.)

LYNNE: Now I did hear something. Quick! Behind that sofa.

(ALFRED swings the picture back into place—but not completely. THEY dash behind the sofa and crouch down. The lights are turned on and GLORIA, in a dressing gown, looks about the room. SHE goes to the picture, notices it's slightly ajar and pushes it against the wall. SHE tries the French doors, takes one last look about the room, shuts the lights and then goes off. After a moment ALFRED and LYNNE come out from behind the sofa.)

ALFRED: Wait here. (*HE goes to the door and looks out.*) It's all right. She's gone.

(LYNNE joins him at the door.)

ALFRED: Let's give her another minute or so.

LYNNE: I won't be able to sleep a wink.

ALFRED: Neither will I? What on earth shall we do?

LYNNE: You really are a wicked man.

ALFRED: Isn't that why you married me? (*HE kisses her.*)

LYNNE: Oh, Freddy, dear, I do love you so.

ALFRED: Quite rightly, too.

LYNNE: We won't ever do this again. Will we?

ALFRED: Ever's a long long time. Come along, my sweet.

(HE takes her by the hand and they go off. A moment later a FIGURE rises from behind the armchair. A flashlight is shone about the room then turned off. The FIGURE goes to the doorway, looks out into the hallway and then goes silently off.)

END OF ACT II, SCENE 1

ACT II

Scene 2

(The following morning. GLORIA enters rapidly, closing the door behind her and picking up the phone.)

GLORIA: Eric? Yes, my dear. No, no, no. They're still here.

(There's a knock on the door.)

GLORIA: Just a moment. (*Back on the phone.*) I can't talk now. I'll call you back. (*SHE hangs up.*) Come in.

(BUSBY enters.)

GLORIA: Mr. Busby. I thought it might be you.

BUSBY: Miss Desmond, I must have a word with you.

GLORIA: I've been given to understand that your car's in working order.

BUSBY: Yes. Yes, it is.

GLORIA: It recovered rather suddenly.

BUSBY: Cars have a way of doing that. Miss Desmond—.

GLORIA: Mr. Busby?

BUSBY: I get the feeling that you've been avoiding me all morning. I'm here to help you. I'm your friend.

GLORIA: Mr. Busby, you are not my friend. You're a mere acquaintance. A ship, I expect, that soon will pass. And, as far as help is concerned, I am perfectly capable of looking after myself.

BUSBY: Under ordinary circumstances I would certainly agree with you. But, unfortunately, you are no match for these arch criminals. These diabolical fiends.

GLORIA: Mr. Busby, what on earth are you talking about?

BUSBY: Do you know who I really am?

GLORIA: You're not Busby Berkely, I know that. Busby Harold?

BUSBY: (*HE removes his wig.*) Now do you know who I am?

GLORIA: Good Lord!

BUSBY: No.

GLORIA: Well, at any rate, it's certainly an improvement. If you're going to wear a wig, my good man, it pays to buy the very best. I can give you the name—.

BUSBY: Miss Desmond. Gloria—.

GLORIA: Gloria?

BUSBY: This is not the time for frivolity.

GLORIA: When that time comes, my good man, I no longer wish to be here.

BUSBY: (*HE removes his mustache.*) Now, do you know who I am?

GLORIA: Whoever you may be—. Whatever you may be I would strongly advise you to continue wearing that mustache. You look absolutely naked without it.

BUSBY: Apparently you never read True Detective. I am Ellery King. The Carter Case. The Case of the Missing Debutante.

GLORIA: Wasn't that Perry Mason? Nero Wolfe? Philo Vance!

BUSBY: It most certainly was not!

GLORIA: Well, you needn't be so vehement about it. Those men are the creme de la creme.

BUSBY: Not in my book they're not.

GLORIA: You're an author, are you?

BUSBY: My dear Miss Desmond, I'm a world famous detective.

GLORIA: Well, I can assure you, sir, that I've done nothing to be ashamed of.

BUSBY: I'm here to help you, Miss Desmond! Don't you understand?!

GLORIA: You really mustn't excite yourself like that. A man of your age. How old are you, incidentally?

BUSBY: Are you deliberately trying to confuse me?

GLORIA: No effort is needed apparently. Fiends! Arch criminals! What on earth are you raving about?

BUSBY: I'm referring to Lady Fortescue—so-called, and that phoney butler. He's no more a butler than I am.

GLORIA: These are serious accusations—from someone I've never met before. Someone I know nothing about.

BUSBY: I've just told you—.

GLORIA: I know what you've just told me. I also know that I have only your word for what you've just told me.

BUSBY: (*HE takes a clipping from his pocket and hands it to her.*) Read this.

GLORIA: What is it?

BUSBY: It's an article from Crime Stories, about the Case of the Missing Shoe.

GLORIA: Is that supposed to be a picture of you?

BUSBY: In disguise.

GLORIA: It's certainly not a very good likeness.

BUSBY: It just so happens to be an excellent likeness. It's the beard that—.

GLORIA: Oh, I like the beard. It's really quite distinguished.

(LYNNE enters in a smart suit.)

LYNNE: Oh, I beg your pardon.

BUSBY: Stay right where you are—Miss Beanbacher. That's right. Miss Myrtle Beanbacher. Alias Gertie Lowenthal. Alias Beatrice Liveright. Alias—.

LYNNE: What on earth is he talking about?

BUSBY: Margaret Hatcher. Alias Jacqueline Kennebunkport, alias Sophie Tuckerworth.

GLORIA: I'm afraid Mr. Busby—.

BUSBY: Mr. King. Mr. Ellery King, detective.

LYNNE: What happened to his hair?

GLORIA: It's right there on the table.

LYNNE: Oh, dear. And that lovely mustache. I thought the mustache was rather dashing.

GLORIA: I quite agree.

(BUSBY pulls at LYNNE's hair and her wig comes off.)

GLORIA: Mr. Busby!

BUSBY: There you are!

GLORIA: I must apologize, Lady Fortescue. It's a lovely wig, by the way. I hope that idiot hasn't damaged it.

BUSBY: Don't you see?

GLORIA: I see quite plainly that you're a very rude man.

LYNNE: And I thought that no one suspected.

BUSBY: Aha!

GLORIA: The man is obviously demented.

(ALFRED enters in sports clothes.)

BUSBY: And here we have the other half of the team.

LYNNE & ALFRED: Team? Team? What team?

BUSBY: The cat burglars of Canarsie. Does that ring a bell? The mythical marauders of Morristown. These two frauds, Miss Desmond, are notorious jewel thieves. I've been on their trail for years. That surprises you, does it not—Mr. Mervyn Hotchkiss, alias Noel Carstairs, alias Henry Irvington, alias Winston Chichester.

ALFRED: What on earth?

BUSBY: Alias the Duke of Dunsinane. Does that ring a bell? Aha!

(HE pulls at ALFRED's hair.)

ALFRED: Ouch! Now why did you do that?

LYNNE: He thinks you're wearing a wig.

ALFRED: Why on earth would I want to wear a wig?

BUSBY: Because you're a master of disguise.

ALFRED: Am I really? A master did you say?

BUSBY: And that woman over there is your mistress.

LYNNE: I beg your pardon, Mr. Busby—.

BUSBY: Mr. King. Mr. Ellery King.

LYNNE: Whatever. It just so happens I am no one's mistress, except, of course—.

BUSBY: Aha!

LYNNE: The mistress of my home, the Dorset Castle.

BUSBY: A likely story.

GLORIA: This woman happens to be my guest.

BUSBY: This woman is a thief. The Hope necklace. The Richmond Tiara. The Dietrich Diamond.

GLORIA: The Dietrich Diamond. Whatever happened to the Dietrich Diamond?

BUSBY: These two are the culprits. They can give you all the particulars. Oh, you two can shrug all you want to, but I've caught you red handed at last.

ALFRED: Where's his hair?

LYNNE: It's right over there on the table.

ALFRED: And his mustache. You really should keep that mustache. You're not a very pretty sight without it.

GLORIA: Thank you so much for your assistance, Alfred, and if you should ever need a letter of recommendation—.

BUSBY: You're not going to let them go. After what I've just told you? (*HE takes an envelope from his pocket.*) Here! Take a look at these.

GLORIA: May I ask what they are?

BUSBY: They're pictures. Pictures of that notorious couple—.

GLORIA: But these don't look like them at all.

BUSBY: Of course, they don't. They're in disguise.

GLORIA: And this one. Their backs are to the camera.

LYNNE & ALFRED: May we see them please?

BUSBY: We?

LYNNE & ALFRED: Yes, of course. Since we're both accused.

GLORIA: May I?

(SHE hands the snapshots to LYNNE who looks at them one by one and hands them to ALFRED.)

BUSBY: You can do what you like with them. I have the negatives.

ALFRED: You're very thorough, I must say—. What did you say your name was?

BUSBY: King. Ellery King. I'm sure you're well acquainted with my name, Mervyn Hotchkiss.

ALFRED: Not really, no. I seldom read pulp fiction. But I shall certainly keep you in mind should I find myself in the need of a detective. But I must say—. What sort of a camera did you use?

BUSBY: A nikon, with a telescopic lens.

ALFRED: I use a little Brownie myself and I must say I get far better results. (*HE hands the pictures back to BUSBY.*) And now, if you have no further use for my services, Miss Desmond, I must be running along. Lady Fortescue, may I give you a lift?

LYNNE: That's very kind of you.

BUSBY: Oh, you're very clever, Mr. Hotchkiss, very clever indeed, but this time the shoe is on the other foot.

ALFRED: A metaphor!

GLORIA: Mr. Busby!

BUSBY: King.

GLORIA: Whatever.

BUSBY: You want proof.

GLORIA: When one accuses one of a crime.

BUSBY: I am well prepared, Miss Desmond, but I'm afraid you shall have to open that safe.

GLORIA: Safe? Safe? What safe?

BUSBY: The safe behind that picture. (*HE swings the picture away from the wall.*) That one there!

GLORIA: Really, Mr. King, Mr. Busby, whatever. You've been spying on me! That's what I get for taking you in off the road. For offering you my hospitality.

BUSBY: I assure you, Miss Desmond, I am in your camp.

GLORIA: That remains to be seen. Everyone turn their back. And I don't want any peeking. Is that understood? Mr. Busby!

BUSBY: King.

GLORIA: Whatever.

BUSBY: Yes. Yes, of course.

(BUSBY, LYNNE and ALFRED turn away and GLORIA opens the safe and removes the jewel case.)

GLORIA: You may turn around. Here you are, Mr. Busby, Mr. King, whatever—you may do the honors.

(BUSBY opens the case.)

GLORIA: Well? Are you satisfied?

BUSBY: That necklace is a fake. It's paste.

GLORIA: How dare you?!

BUSBY: I regret to inform you, Miss Desmond, but you've been duped.

GLORIA: It's quite possible, my dear, that you are the dupe.

BUSBY: Examine that necklace. Examine it carefully.

GLORIA: I shall do nothing of the sort. I know the Mandarin necklace when I see it.

BUSBY: Then I shall examine it for you. (*HE examines the necklace carefully, then takes out his jewelers magnifying glass and continues the examination.*)

GLORIA: Well, are you satisfied?

BUSBY: There must be some mistake.

GLORIA: Obviously, and I think you owe these people an apology, don't you?

BUSBY: Not so fast. Apparently they were prepared for this and they've retrieved the imitation and they plan, no doubt, to return at a later date. If you'll examine these people's bags—.

LYNNE: Really!

ALFRED: This is really too much!

BUSBY: Have you any objection to being searched?

ALFRED: None whatsoever. Proceed. (*HE holds up his hands.*)

LYNNE: And me as well. (*SHE holds up her hands.*)

BUSBY: I was referring to your luggage.

GLORIA: Very well, if you insist. Alfred!

BUSBY: I'll fetch it myself. Their luggage is in the hallway. Right outside that door.

ALFRED: This is unspeakable!

GLORIA: Surely you have nothing to hide, my dear.

ALFRED: No. No, of course not. But—.

LYNNE: It's the principle.

ALFRED: Yes, yes, of course it's the principle.

BUSBY: Is it, indeed? (*HE goes off.*)

GLORIA: Gently, children, gently.

(BUSBY returns with two overnight bags.)

GLORIA: Proceed, Mr. Busby, Mr. King, whatever.

(BUSBY empties the contents of one bag, examines the inside of the bag, then turns the bag upside down.)

GLORIA: Well?

BUSBY: Let's have a look at Lady Fortescue's bag.

GLORIA: Calmly, my dear, calmly.

ALFRED: If there's no objection I should like to repack my bag.

GLORIA: Don't you think you owe Alfred an apology Mr. Busby, Mr. King, whatever.

BUSBY: Let's wait and see.

ALFRED: May I repack my bag?

BUSBY: You may.

(ALFRED repacks his bag. BUSBY picks up LYNNE's bag and places it on the table.)

GLORIA: Proceed, Mr. Busby, Mr. King, whatever.

(BUSBY empties the second bag, examines the inside of the bag and turns it upside down.) Well?

BUSBY: It's on their person.

LYNNE: Would you like us to strip?

GLORIA: That won't be necessary. I should like to examine your bag, Mr. Busby, Mr. King, whatever.

BUSBY: My bag?

GLORIA: Unless you have some objection.

BUSBY: Most certainly not.

ALFRED: I'll do the honors this time. (*HE goes off.*)

LYNNE: May I?

BUSBY: Yes. Yes, of course.

(LYNNE repacks her bag.)

GLORIA: I must apologize, Lady Fortescue.

LYNNE: The man is obviously deranged.

(ALFRED returns with an overnight bag.)

ALFRED: May I?

GLORIA: Please do.

(ALFRED empties the contents then turns the bag upside down.)

BUSBY: Aha!

ALFRED: (*HE feels inside the bag.*) What's this?

BUSBY: It's a secret pocket, where I keep certain papers.

ALFRED: This doesn't feel like papers to me. May I?

BUSBY: Those are private papers.

ALFRED: I'm a very slow reader.

GLORIA: Surely you have no objection, Mr. Busby, Mr. King, whatever.

BUSBY: Of course not, so long as those documents remain unread.

(ALFRED reaches into the bag and pulls out the necklace.)

BUSBY: I should have known. These people will stop at nothing. That necklace was planted there, on purpose. I can assure you, Miss Desmond, my reputation is impeccable. I have all sorts of letters of reference. The King of Belgium. The Duchess of Parma! It's a plot, don't you see? It's a fraud. They were planning this all along.

GLORIA: You mean they saw through your disguise.

BUSBY: Yes, yes, yes!

GLORIA: They've been expecting you.

BUSBY: Exactly.

GLORIA: They knew that your car would break down in front of my house.

BUSBY: I know it seems far fetched, but these two are the devils incarnate. Why in the case of the Deitrich Diamond they posed as plumbers.

LYNNE: Plumbers, you say?

BUSBY: Yes, plumbers!

ALFRED: I assure you, Mr. Busby.

BUSBY: Mr. King.

ALFRED: Whatever.

LYNNE & ALFRED: We know nothing about plumbing.

LYNNE: I wouldn't know a pipe—

ALFRED: From a plunger.

BUSBY: And in the case of the Richmond tiara they posed as Tasmanian royalty.

LYNNE: Upper?

ALFRED: Or lower?

GLORIA: Does this necklace belong to you or does it not?

BUSBY: It most certainly does not.

GLORIA: Then I fully intend to take possession of it.

BUSBY: Please do.

GLORIA: And I shall not press charges, for the sake of your mother. You do have a mother, don't you?

BUSBY: I assure you, Miss Desmond, I do. I do. And a father, as well.

GLORIA: I should hope so, my dear man. You may repack your things.

BUSBY: Thank you. (*HE begins to repack his bag.*)

GLORIA: And, if you don't mind, I shall restore my necklace to its proper place.

BUSBY: Please do.

(As BUSBY continues to repack GLORIA picks up the paste necklace and puts it into the case.)

ALFRED: But—.

(LYNNE pulls on his sleeve to silence him.)

GLORIA: Alfred.

(SHE hands him the case.)

ALFRED: Yes. Yes, of course.

(ALFRED places the case in the safe, locks the safe and replaces the picture.)

GLORIA: Thank you, my dear. And now, Mr. Busby, Mr. King, whatever, I think you owe these people an apology.

BUSBY: Never!

LYNNE: That's quite all right. As a matter of fact, it restores one's faith in humanity to find someone so upright, so dedicated to uphold the cause of truth and justice.

ALFRED: Law and order.

LYNNE: Just so.

BUSBY: And if you think you've heard the last of me, Myrtle Beanbacher and Mervyn Hotchkiss, you are both, very much mistaken. I take it, Miss Desmond, I am free to go.

GLORIA: Unless, of course, these people prefer to press charges.

BUSBY: Charges? Charges? What sort of charges?

GLORIA: Slander, my dear, is a very serious offense.

LYNNE & ALFRED: No, no, no, no, no!

BUSBY: My apologies to you, Miss Desmond. And paste or not, I'd keep an eye on that necklace while these two are afoot.

GLORIA: Thank you for the warning, Mr. Busby, Mr. King, whatever. And as far as the Mandarin Necklace is concerned, it is heavily insured. And though I should be devastated by its loss the insurance would go a long way to pay some outstanding debts. Have you anything further to say, Mr. Busby, Mr. King, whatever?

BUSBY: Nothing but this. There is no place for an honest man in this world. (*HE picks up his bag and starts off.*)

LYNNE: Oh, Mr. Busby.

BUSBY: Mr. King.

LYNNE: Whatever. Your wig.

BUSBY: I won't be needing that Lady Fortescue. For when we meet again, I shall be wearing a disguise that is impenetrable. (*HE goes off.*)

GLORIA: If you'll excuse me. (*SHE goes off.*)

ALFRED: Dare we?

LYNNE: I think we're expected to.

ALFRED: Well, I'm certainly not one to disappoint a lady.

(ALFRED pops the necklace into his bag. GLORIA reenters.)

GLORIA: There's nothing so unpleasant as a righteous man who's so terribly—

LYNNE: Righteous.

GLORIA: Exactly. Thank you, my dears.

ALFRED & LYNNE: Thank you, Miss Desmond.

GLORIA: May I ask how old you are?

ALFRED & LYNNE: Thirty three.

GLORIA: That's just the age of my missing child would have been. Were you really born in China?

ALFRED: Chinatown, I'm afraid. Was your missing child a boy or a girl?

GLORIA: I never knew. You may kiss me good-bye.

(SHE extends her face. LYNNE kisses her on one cheek while ALFRED kisses her on the other. THEY start off.)

GLORIA: Oh, and Lady Fortescue.

LYNNE: Miss Desmond?

GLORIA: Gloria. If you should happen to run into Eric this afternoon, please give him my regards.

LYNNE: Why, yes. I most certainly will.

(LYNNE goes off followed by ALFRED. GLORIA heaves a sigh. SHE picks up the phone and dials.)

GLORIA: Eric? They were absolutely splendid. How much are we giving them? Let's make it fifty. I mean, after all, it is insured for over a million. Yes. Yes, I'll call them now. (*SHE hangs up and dials the operator.*) Yes, my dear—. Can you give me the number of Lloyds of London.

(While SHE waits for the response SHE hums "I'll See You Again.")

CURTAIN

THE DESERTER

A Play in One Act

CAST OF CHARACTERS

The Soldier
The Sergeant
The Priest

SCENE

A deserted chateau in Europe, one winter morning early in 1945. The furniture and French windows are covered with dust cloths.

(A winter morning early in 1945. The furniture in the room and the French windows are covered with dust cloths. A SOLDIER enters the room, handcuffed and unarmed, followed by a SERGEANT, armed with a pistol and a rifle. The SERGEANT carries a lighted candle.)

SOLDIER: It's dark in here.

SERGEANT: I've got some more candles. Just stay where you are. (*HE sets down the candle and lights two more.*) It should be getting light pretty soon.

SOLDIER: Will I get a paper and pencil?

SERGEANT: The Corporal went to get you some. You want something to eat?

(The SOLDIER shakes his head.)

SERGEANT: You can sit down if you want to. Why don't you stop sniveling?

SOLDIER: I've got a cold.

SERGEANT: Well, there's no place to light a fire here.

SOLDIER: There's a fireplace over there.

SERGEANT: Well, there ain't no wood. Besides, we ain't gonna be here long, anyway.

SOLDIER: How much time is there?

SERGEANT: About an hour.

SOLDIER: I wanna write my wife a letter. She doesn't even know what's happening to me.

SERGEANT: You'll get your paper and pencil.

SOLDIER: The Corporal doesn't know what room we're in.

SERGEANT: Don't worry. He'll find us. Were you really in jail?

SOLDIER: Yeah. A couple of years. I was only eighteen.

SERGEANT: What were you in for?

SOLDIER: Robbery.

SERGEANT: What'd you steal?

SOLDIER: Not very much. The first time, you mean? I was out on parole and we took a car.

SERGEANT: You were really a tough character, weren't you?

SOLDIER: I was pretty mixed up. You ain't had much sleep.

SERGEANT: Don't worry about me.

SOLDIER: Riding all night. Where are we?

SERGEANT: What difference does it make?

SOLDIER: I just wanted to know, that's all.

SERGEANT: Well, I don't even know the name of the place. We're out in the country somewhere. We got this whole place all to ourselves. That shows you how important you are.

SOLDIER: I never wanted to be this important.

SERGEANT: Yeah, you thought you could get away with it.

SOLDIER: I ain't never got away with anything in all my life. My wife is very sick.

SERGEANT: What's the matter with her?

SOLDIER: She gets these spells and she's got diabetes.

SERGEANT: Well, that's not serious.

SOLDIER: It can be. What with one thing or another.

SERGEANT: Well, she'll get your pension.

SOLDIER: I don't know if I'll get a pension. She will, that is. I mean, it's not as if I was killed in action or anything like that.

SERGEANT: No, it ain't. You poor son-of-a-bitch! At least you had a chance fighting the Germans.

SOLDIER: They ain't never shot anybody before.

SERGEANT: And that's what you were counting on.

SOLDIER: If only. . . .

SERGEANT: If only what?

SOLDIER: It's this waiting.

SERGEANT: Suppose we had shot you on the way, like you wanted us to. You'd never have gotten a chance to write to your wife.

SOLDIER: Are you . . . ?

SERGEANT: Am I what?

SOLDIER: Are you gonna be on . . . the firing squad?

SERGEANT: No.

SOLDIER: How many?

SERGEANT: Twelve. One of the guns has a blank.

SOLDIER: Suppose I don't die on the first volley?

SERGEANT: Then they fire again. Don't worry. These men are good shots.

SOLDIER: They say before you die, you're supposed to remember everything. I don't remember anything. All I can think about is my wife being left all alone.

SERGEANT: You should have thought of that before.

SOLDIER: This is a nice room. All them books. I never did much reading, but I always planned to. Except, of course, when I was in prison. I did a lot of reading then. It wasn't really a prison though. It was a reformatory, because I was so young. I should have never left that place. There were lots of times that I wished I was back there. This is one of them. What was that?

SERGEANT: I didn't hear anything.

SOLDIER: I thought I heard someone. I suppose this ain't no fun for you.

SERGEANT: It's my job. In the army you do what you're told.

SOLDIER: It's the same way in reformatory. I think I'm gonna be sick.

SERGEANT: How many times can you be sick in one night? You ain't got nothin' to throw up anymore.

SOLDIER: You believe in heaven and hell?

SERGEANT: I don't know. I never think about it much. Do you?

SOLDIER: I'm Catholic. I never went to church that much, but I guess I'm still a Catholic. My wife ain't though. I got this picture of her. They let me keep it. I want to be buried with it.

SERGEANT: Yeah, she's nice lookin'.

SOLDIER: She ain't really pretty. What you might call pretty, I mean. But she's the most beautiful person I've ever known in all my life. And she's the only reason . . . I mean, I don't care about the rest of it. I mean, where does it get you? We ain't got nothin', and we both worked hard. We was just beginning to make it when I got drafted. I guess it's too late for any kind of a pardon. In the movies they all come at the last minute. My wife and I used to go to the movies twice a week, at least. I never thought they'd send me overseas. I was "4 F." Are you married?

SERGEANT: No.

SOLDIER: Have you got a special girl?

SERGEANT: I gotta lot of special girls.

SOLDIER: I mean back home.

SERGEANT: A couple.

SOLDIER: I used to play around a little. Not that I was ever a great one with the ladies. My wife changed my whole life, you know. I never thought I'd make it. Out in the world, I mean, and I never would have, if it hadn't been for her. I really thought we were gonna make it. I guess I should have known better. I went to a fortune teller once. She told me a lot of lies. I never could figure out whether she was holding something back from me or not. Do you believe in fortune-tellers?

SERGEANT: No. They're a lot of crap.

SOLDIER: Sometimes they're right though. This one we went to. She was right about a couple of things. She said I was gonna take a long trip.

SERGEANT: That's what they all say.

SOLDIER: My parents used to drink a lot and they used to fight all the time. My brother and I never used to have enough to eat. That's why we started stealing in the first place. Just to get something to eat.

SERGEANT: You don't have to steal to get something to eat.

SOLDIER: If you're a kid, you do.

SERGEANT: You think the Germans are our friends?

SOLDIER: No, it wasn't that.

SERGEANT: What was it then? I mean, everybody's scared. Anybody that's got any sense. But now that you're here, what have you got to lose?

SOLDIER: I just couldn't.

SERGEANT: Couldn't what?

SOLDIER: I guess I'm just sick, that's all. I ought to be put away somewhere. I told them that, before they sent me over. I never was much of anything. I wasn't even a good crook. I was the one that always got caught.

SERGEANT: I mean, you heard them shooting at you. They were out to kill you. If you were in my squad, I would have shot you right then and there.

SOLDIER: I told the captain back in the States. I told the captain. I said, "Captain Blaine, I don't know if I can kill anybody."

SERGEANT: The war's almost over. A couple more months. That's all that's left. A couple more months. What would you do if a German was standing in front of you with a gun? What would you do?

SOLDIER: I don't know.

SERGEANT: Then you might as well be dead because that's what would have happened to you anyway. Suppose they shot your buddy, standing right next to you? What would you do?

SOLDIER: I don't know. I don't know!!

SERGEANT: Okay, okay.

SOLDIER: I want that paper and pencil.

SERGEANT: You still got plenty of time. Just take it easy. I think you're stupid, that's all.

SOLDIER: I guess I must be.

SERGEANT: Well, crying ain't gonna help you any.

SOLDIER: I can't help it.

SERGEANT: Well, go ahead and cry then. (*After a moment.*) What'd you do, just walk away?

SOLDIER: We got separated from our outfit, this buddy of mine and me. We didn't know where they were, so we just joined this other outfit. An English outfit.

SERGEANT: You didn't try to find your own company.

SOLDIER: Well, we did ask a couple of people, but nobody seemed to know anything.

SERGEANT: You didn't ask any officer, did you?

SOLDIER: We spoke to a lieutenant. But then we did rejoin our outfit. I told them I was sick. I told them I couldn't kill anybody. I asked them to send me back somewhere. Anywhere. I wasn't gonna fire my rifle. I begged that captain. I mean the one over here. I told him, "I'm not gonna kill anybody. I'm warning you. You gotta send me back." But he wouldn't listen to me. He assigned me to this company. He told me I gotta stay there . . . and I left.

SERGEANT: And they caught up with you.

SOLDIER: I gave myself up.

SERGEANT: You didn't even have the guts to run away. You thought we were gonna put you in the stockade and take care of you to the end of the war. Didn't you?

SOLDIER: They ain't never shot anybody before. Not even in the last war. They ain't never shot anybody.

SERGEANT: They've been waitin' for you.

SOLDIER: I guess they have. I would like to speak to a priest.

SERGEANT: Don't worry. You'll speak to a priest.

SOLDIER: A Catholic priest.

SERGEANT: They know you're Catholic, don't they?

SOLDIER: I guess so.

SERGEANT: Then you'll speak to a Catholic priest.

SOLDIER: I don't know what he'll say about my being married to a non-Catholic. We used to go to church together. A Catholic church, and she did agree to raise our children Catholic. But we weren't married in a Roman Catholic church.

SERGEANT: Why not?

SOLDIER: My parents baptized me in the wrong church. I don't know how it happened, so the priest wouldn't marry us. But I've always been a Catholic.

SERGEANT: I don't think it makes much difference anymore.

SOLDIER: The church is very strict about these things. We were planning on having a baby. We had a beautiful apartment when I left. But my wife had to give it up because she got sick and I was in the army and there wasn't enough money to pay the rent and the furniture wasn't all paid for. What day is today?

SERGEANT: It's Wednesday. Maybe there's some paper around here somewhere. You just sit there. I'll look around. There sure are plenty of books. Here's some paper for you. Pretty fancy, too. It's even got your initial on it. Here's some ink and here's a pen. You can write on this table here.

(The SOLDIER extends his hand-cuffed wrists.)

SERGEANT: Just a minute. (*HE places the writing equipment on a table and then removes the handcuffs.*) Okay. But I gotta put 'em back on as soon as you're finished.

SOLDIER: (*HE begins to write.*) My Dearest . . . (*HE turns to the SERGEANT.*) This pen isn't very good.

SERGEANT: (*HE goes to the secretary.*) Here's another one.

SOLDIER: Thank you. (*HE tears up the sheet and starts another.*) My Dearest, This is the last letter you will ever receive from me. I know this will come as quite a shock to you, as I haven't written to you about the trouble I've been in. I was waiting to see how it would come out. As I told you, I would never fire my rifle, and I haven't. I can't tell you how terrible it is here. You will probably receive an official letter from the army, telling you that I have been executed for desertion, and I did. And I would do it again. This war is a terrible thing. When we rolled into Germany the first day, I was sick, and I've been sick ever since. There were bodies all along the road. It's not like in the movies, I'll tell you that. You must be patient with your family. They're older people and they're used to having their own way; and you mustn't think that because I'm gone this is the end of your life, because it isn't. You are still young and although you are having trouble with your health right now, I am sure you will come out all right. It's going to be hard for you, I know, going on alone, and you mustn't be sad about me. I was born under an unlucky star. I think my whole family was, but my troubles will soon be over. There's only been one good thing in my life and that was you. I never thought I could be so happy on this earth. Your love has made everything worthwhile for me. I carry your picture in my pocket and I've asked that it be buried with me and they promised me they would. (*HE turns to the SERGEANT.*) What time is it?

SERGEANT: You still got half an hour.

SOLDIER: (*HE continues to write.*) There's not much more to say. I wish now that I hadn't stopped writing to you because there are so many things I would like to have told you about, but I've forgotten most of them and somehow they don't seem very important now. The important thing is now for you to be happy. I know that's easy to say, but you are strong; much stronger than me, and you will survive. I don't think you will be entitled to any pension because of the circumstances, but I think you ought to look into it because you never can tell. I hope some day you will meet someone; someone who understands you as I did, and someone who can take care of you, because you deserve the best. I shall always be grateful for the love you have given me. Please say good-bye to my brother for me, and I would appreciate it if you would write to him every once in a while. Life can be very lonely in prison. I kiss you for the last time, my dearest darling. Your loving husband . . . Always. (*HE turns to the SERGEANT.*) What about an envelope?

SERGEANT: I didn't see any there. Write the address on the back. We'll find an envelope for it.

SOLDIER: (*HE folds the letter and writes the address.*) I think someone's coming. It isn't time yet, is it?

SERGEANT: No.

(A PRIEST enters in a captain's uniform, carrying a knapsack. The SERGEANT salutes him and the PRIEST returns the salute.)

PRIEST: I'm Father Murray. I'd like to be alone with the prisoner.

SERGEANT: Yes, sir. I'd better put his handcuffs back on.

PRIEST: That won't be necessary.

SERGEANT: I just took them off so that he could write a letter to his wife.

PRIEST: I'll be responsible for him.

SERGEANT: Yes, Sir.

PRIEST: Let us know when they're ready.

SERGEANT: Yes, Sir. (*HE salutes and goes off.*)

SOLDIER: I'd like to confess, Father.

PRIEST: That's what I'm here for, Son. I'll be with you from now on. Just let me set things up first.

SOLDIER: That's a letter to my wife. I don't have any envelope, so I wrote the address on the back.

PRIEST: I'll see that she gets it. (*HE folds the letter and puts it into his pocket. HE then removes a cloth from his knapsack and spreads the cloth on the table. HE takes a prayer book from the knapsack and then from his pocket the container holding the wafer. HE drapes a purple stole around his shoulders and turns to the SOLDIER.*) All right, Son.

SOLDIER: I must tell you, Father, I wasn't married in the church.

PRIEST: Why not?

SOLDIER: My wife isn't Catholic, but she agreed to raise our children Catholic, and I was raised as a Roman Catholic, but then I found out that my parents baptized me in the wrong church and Father Donavan refused to marry us.

PRIEST: You were baptized though.

SOLDIER: Yes, Father.

PRIEST: And you have been a practicing Catholic.

SOLDIER: Yes, Father.

PRIEST: Then I will accept your confession.

SOLDIER: (*HE kneels and crosses himself.*) Bless me, Father, for I have sinned. It's been eight months since my last confession and these are my sins. I have not attended mass on Sunday for several months. I have had impure thoughts and I have abused myself. I have listened to dirty jokes and took part in obscene discussions. I have used the Lord's name in vain. I have refused to obey my superiors. When the Captain told me I had to join Company "G" I told him that I wouldn't, and when he said I had to, I ran away. And I ran away before that.

PRIEST: Why did you do that?

SOLDIER: I was afraid, Father. I was afraid of being shot.

PRIEST: And do you think that the rest of us aren't afraid?

SOLDIER: I told the Captain in the States, Father, I told Captain Blaine I was sick. I couldn't kill anybody.

PRIEST: We are fighting a war. You love your country, don't you? And your wife and your family?

SOLDIER: Yes, Father. I love my wife very much.

PRIEST: You're here to protect her and all the blessings that you've received from your country.

SOLDIER: I know that, Father. But why couldn't I have been assigned to another job?

PRIEST: That's not for you to question. In the army you're supposed to do as you're told. That's the only way an army can be run.

SOLDIER: I know that, Father.

PRIEST: And yet you deliberately defied your officers.

SOLDIER: It's only because I was afraid, Father.

PRIEST: That's not a good enough reason.

SOLDIER: Father, please . . . My parents were rotten. They were no good. I've hated them all my life. And they never cared about me or my brother. We spent most of our life in the street, when we were kids. My brother's in jail right now because of them and I would be, too, if I hadn't met my wife.

PRIEST: But you did. And you've let her down.

SOLDIER: Father . . .

PRIEST: Yes? What is it?

SOLDIER: My brother's in prison because he took part in a robbery where someone was killed. I used to carry a gun, not that I ever thought I'd use it. But I thought that I was entitled to something in this life. And then when my brother took part in this robbery I had a long talk with Father Hart at the reformatory. He said there was no excuse for killing anybody. Murder is murder, no matter what reason you had, and it was a mortal sin. I know this is different, but somehow I got it into my head that it was wrong to carry a gun. I was a terrible shot in training. I know I'm all mixed up, Father, but then when I saw all those dead Germans. Somebody killed them, I thought, and that was wrong. And I couldn't get that out of my head, and I got nauseous just at the idea of firing my rifle. And then when we were attacked, something in me just froze, and I knew it was all wrong. My being here, I mean. I should be back somewhere else, because I was no good as a soldier, and I ran, Father. I guess I could have found my outfit if I had really wanted to, but they'd want me to fight.

PRIEST: And what about those other soldiers? Your comrades? Did you ever think that you were letting them down? Did you ever think that they had to do your fighting for you? Did you ever think that some of them might be alive right now, if you had been fighting beside them?

SOLDIER: I was never a very good shot.

PRIEST: We all have responsibilities and you have shirked your responsibilities.

SOLDIER: I should be home, taking care of my wife. She needs me. She's a sick woman.

PRIEST: Your country needs you, or it did.

SOLDIER: But why me, Father? Why me?

PRIEST: Because you're a man. Because we don't get anything in this life for nothing. Freedom is something you have to fight for. You've enjoyed the benefits of your country, haven't you?

SOLDIER: Yes, Sir.

PRIEST: Then you are in debt to your country, just as you are in debt to your parents for giving you life, and just as you are in debt to the Lord for permitting you to enjoy that life. And a debt must be paid eventually.

SOLDIER: But why did Father Hart tell me that it was wrong to kill? He said there was no excuse for killing anyone. None whatsoever. He said he understood that there could be reasons for it, but there was no excuse.

PRIEST: This is war, boy. God doesn't want you to sit on your heels and let your enemy destroy you.

SOLDIER: I've always been weak, Father. I've never really had any guts. Not for anything. Maybe I'm better off dead.

PRIEST: We're all waiting for the Lord to receive us.

SOLDIER: Maybe I'm lucky, Father. I know when it's gonna happen.

PRIEST: It will happen very quickly, and Paradise is forever.

SOLDIER: Oh, Father. (*HE weeps.*)

PRIEST: I want you to go out there and show those men you are not afraid. I will be with you and the Lord will be with you. You will not be alone. Are you truly sorry for all your sins and are you ready to face death with a true spirit of repentance?

SOLDIER: I am, Father.

PRIEST: I want you to say an Our Father, a Hail Mary and a Glory be.

SOLDIER: I'm not sure that I remember them.

PRIEST: I'll help you.

SOLDIER: Yes, Father.

PRIEST: I absolve you of all your sins in the name of (*Crossing himself.*) the Father, and of the Son and of the Holy Ghost. Amen.

SOLDIER: Amen. O my God, I am heartily sorry for having offended you, and I detest all my sins.

PRIEST: May almighty God have mercy on you, forgive your sins and bring you to everlasting life. Amen.

SOLDIER: Our Father who art in heaven, hallowed be thy name . . .

PRIEST: Thy kingdom come . . .

SOLDIER: Thy kingdom come . . .

PRIEST: Thy will be done . . .

SOLDIER: Thy will be done . . . on earth . . .

PRIEST: As it is in heaven.

SOLDIER: As it is in heaven. Forgive us our trespasses . . .

PRIEST: Give us this day . . .

SOLDIER: Give us this day our daily bread . . .

PRIEST: Forgive us our trespasses . . .

SOLDIER: Forgive us our trespasses . . .

PRIEST: As we forgive those who trespass against us.

SOLDIER: As we forgive those who trespass against us.

PRIEST: And lead us not into temptation . . .

SOLDIER: And lead us not into temptation . . . and deliver us from evil. Amen.

PRIEST: Amen.

SOLDIER: Hail Mary, full of Grace, the Lord is with thee . . .

PRIEST: Blessed . . .

SOLDIER: Blessed art thou amongst women and blessed is the fruit of thy womb, Jesus.

PRIEST: Holy Mary . . .

SOLDIER: Holy Mary, mother of God, pray for us sinners, now and at the hour of our death. Amen.

PRIEST: Amen.

SOLDIER: Glory be to the Father, to the Son, and to the Holy Ghost . . .

PRIEST: As it was . . .

SOLDIER: As it was in the beginning and ever shall be, world without end. Amen.

PRIEST: Amen. (*HE removes the wafer from the container.*) Corpus domini nostri Jesu Christe custodiat animam tuam in vitam eternam. Amen.

SOLDIER: Amen.

(The PRIEST places the wafer on the SOLDIER's tongue. The SOLDIER swallows the wafer, crosses himself and rises.)

PRIEST: Sit down, Son. They will come for us when they're ready.

SOLDIER: Will they cover my eyes?

PRIEST: Your eyes will be covered. They'll place a black hood over your head. You'll be tied to a post.

SOLDIER: Where will they do it?

PRIEST: There's a beautiful garden in back of the chateau. Of course, it's covered with snow now.

SOLDIER: Have you spoken to the men on the firing squad?

PRIEST: Yes.

SOLDIER: How do they feel about it?

PRIEST: They feel very bad about it. But I told them they were doing their duty and God expects that of every man.

SOLDIER: I want you to tell them that I don't hold anything against them.

PRIEST: I will, Son. And you're not to think about the execution. That will only be a matter of seconds. You're to think about Paradise.

SOLDIER: Yes, Father, I will. Somehow, I knew in my bones this was going to happen to me. I guess they had to make an example of someone and I am an ex-con, so why not me? That's the way it's always been.

PRIEST: It's the will of God; and when you get up there, Son, I want you to say a little prayer for me.

SOLDIER: I will, Father. I'll pray that you won't be joining me too soon. And be sure to tell the men on the firing squad. . . .

PRIEST: I will, Son.

SOLDIER: You don't have to worry about me, Father. I'm not afraid anymore, because I know that my suffering is almost over. I feel sorry for all the rest of the men who gotta go on fighting in this war. They'll never know when they're gonna get it. It was the waiting and the uncertainty that was the worst of it. How many people are gonna be out there, Father?

PRIEST: Maybe eighty or so.

SOLDIER: Well, I ain't gonna break down. Will you write a letter to my wife, Father, and tell her that when I went that I was at peace?

PRIEST: I will, Son.

SOLDIER: How much more time is there?

PRIEST: Any minute now.

(The SERGEANT enters, a little unsteadily, and salutes. The SOLDIER rises.)

SERGEANT: They're ready, Father. They're waiting outside.

PRIEST: Thank you, Sergeant. Come along, Son.

SOLDIER: Thank you, Sergeant Garrel. (*HE extends his hand and shakes hands with the SERGEANT.*)

PRIEST: I'll be back for my things, Sergeant. You can just leave them there.

(The SOLDIER starts off slowly, his lips moving in silent prayer. The PRIEST follows him, carrying the prayer book.)

PRIEST: Jesus, Mary and Joseph, bless us now at the hour of our death. O Lord, my God, whatever manner of death is pleasing to thee, with all its anguish, pains and sorrows, I now accept from thy hand with a resigned and willing spirit.

(It is broad daylight now. The SERGEANT salutes the empty doorway, then draws a half empty cognac bottle from his jacket, and takes a healthy swig, concealing the bottle in his jacket. HE puts the stationary, ink and pens back in the secretary, then gathers up the candles, after blowing them out. HE looks at the things the PRIEST has left on the table, then puts them in Father Murray's knapsack, which HE slings over his shoulder. Martial music is heard softly in the distance as the SERGEANT goes off unsteadily. A volley of shots is heard and the martial music swells.)

CURTAIN

THE DESERTER
was inspired by and is dedicated to the memory of Private Eddie D. Slovik, who was shot for desertion on January 31, 1945.

PHOTO BY MARTY BEIM

About the Author

As an actor, Norman Beim has appeared on Broadway in "Inherit the Wind" with the legendary Paul Muni, Off Broadway at Joe Papp's Public Theatre, and stood by for Van Johnson in the national tour of "Tribute." Among his directing credits is a production of "Harvey" with Joe E. Brown. His plays have been produced in Holland, Belgium, and at various theatres across the country, and have won a number of awards. Mr. Beim is a member of the Dramatists Guild.